Streamline ENGLISH

BERNARD HARTLEY & PETER VINEY

DESTINATIONS

An intensive English course for
intermediate students

Oxford University Press

Oxford University Press
Walton Street, Oxford OX2 6DP

Oxford New York Toronto
Delhi Bombay Calcutta Madras Karachi
Petaling Jaya Singapore Hong Kong Tokyo
Nairobi Dar es Salaam Cape Town
Melbourne Auckland
and associated companies in
Berlin Ibadan

OXFORD and OXFORD ENGLISH
are trade marks of Oxford University Press

ISBN 0 19 432227 0 (student's edition)
ISBN 0 19 432228 9 (teacher's edition)
ISBN 0 19 432229 7 (set of two cassettes)
© Bernard Hartley and Peter Viney 1979

First published in this edition 1979
Eighteenth impression 1991

Illustrations by:

Alan Austin	Paddy Mounter
Stephen Crisp	Terry Pastor
Julian Graddon	Gary Rees
Alun Hood	Elly Robinson
Alan Lawrence	Bill Sanderson
Edward McLachlan	Brian Sweet
Brian Moore	Ken Thompson
Richard Morris	

Photographs by:

Vernon Brooke	Terry Williams
Billett Potter	

The publishers would like to thank the following for their time and assistance:

R. R. Alden & Son Ltd	House of Tweed, Oxford
Barclays Bank Ltd	Luna Caprese Restaurant
Bollom Ltd	New Theatre, Oxford
Boots The Chemists	Oxford Illustrators Ltd
Glyn Brown	H. Samuel Ltd
Charmers Hair Craft	J. Summersell
City of Oxford Motor	Sunshine Records
Services Ltd	Thames Valley Police
Debenhams	

The publishers would like to thank the following for permission to reproduce photographs:
All-Sport Photographic Ltd
Pat Brindley
British Airways
Photographic Department, B L Cars, Cowley
British Petroleum Co Ltd
Lance Brown
Colour Library International Ltd
Colorific Photo Library
Colorsport
Gerry Cranham
Mary Evans Picture Library
Alan Hutchison Library
Keystone Press Agency Ltd
London Features International Ltd
The Mansell Collection
Paul Popper Ltd
Rolls Royce Motors Ltd
Syndication International Ltd
The Times Newspapers Ltd

Set in Palatino and Helvetica by
Filmtype Services Limited, Scarborough
Printed in Belgium

CONTENTS

ARRIVALS

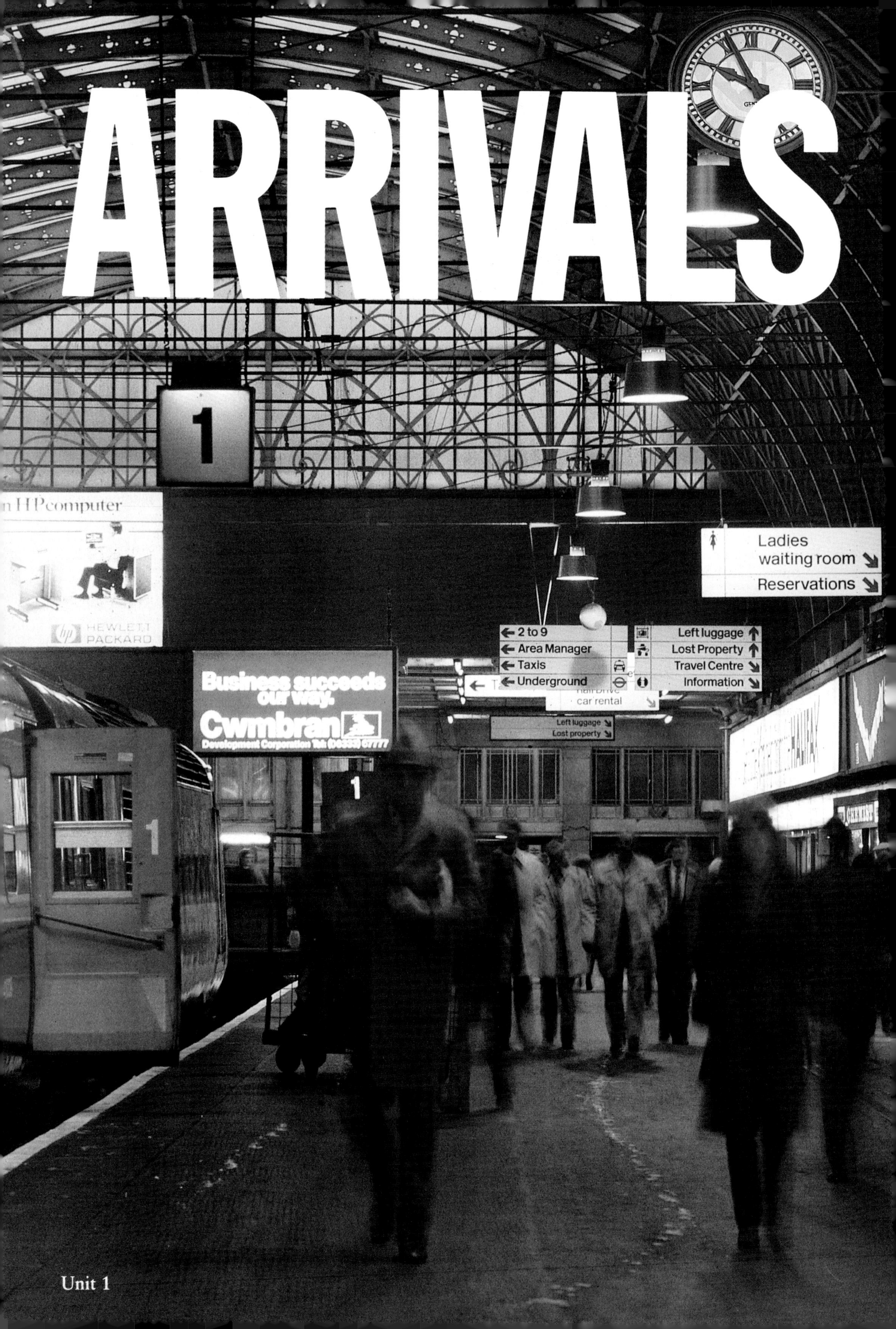

1

Ladies
waiting room ↘
Reservations ↘

← 2 to 9   Left luggage ↑
← Area Manager   Lost Property ↑
← Taxis   Travel Centre ↘
← Underground   Information ↘

car rental

Left luggage ↘
Lost property ↘

Unit 1

Trains **No entry**

A Excuse me ... Mr Ward?
B Yes?
A I'm Charles Archer, from Continental Computers. How do you do?
B How do you do? Thank you for coming to meet us.
A Not at all. Did you have a good trip?
B Yes, thank you. Oh, I'd like you to meet Philip Mason. He's our sales manager.
A How do you do?

Exercise 1
A Mrs Bond?
B ....
A I'm Steven Robson, from Anglo Exports. How do you do?
B ....
A That's all right. Did you have a nice journey?
B ....
A Oh, may I introduce John Benson? He's our financial director.
B ....

C Sarah!
D Hi.
C Hi. I haven't seen you for ages. How's things?
D All right. And you?
C Fine. How's work?
D OK. Do you fancy a coffee?
C Oh, yes, I'd love one.

E Hello, Dorothy.
F Hello, Margaret. How are you?
E Very well, thanks, and you?
F Oh, I'm fine. How's the family?
E They're all fine. My car's just outside the station. Shall I take one of your bags?
F Oh, yes ... thank you.

G Good morning.
H Good morning.
G Single to Exeter, please.
H £14.70, please.
G There you are. Thank you ... er ... what time's the next train?
H 10.25.
G Thank you.

Exercise 2
Look at the conversation between G and H, and practise two similar conversations, one for Exeter St David's, and one for Penzance.

Rail Fares	Exeter St David's	Penzance
Single	£14.70	£25.80
Return	£23.40	£47.90
Cheap day return*	£17.40	£28.10

*You must return on the same day.

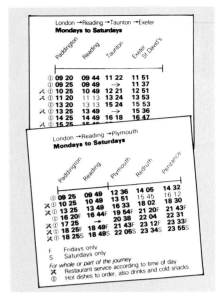

London →Reading →Taunton →Exeter Mondays to Saturdays			
Paddington	Reading	Taunton	Exeter St David's
① 09 20	09 44	11 22	11 51
① 09 25	09 49	→	11 37
✕① 10 25	10 49	12 21	12 51
✕① 11 20	11 13	13 24	13 53
① 13 20	13 13	15 24	15 53
✕① 13 25	13 49	→	15 36
① 14 25	14 49	16 18	16 47
✕① 15 25	15		

London →Reading →Plymouth Mondays to Saturdays				
Paddington	Reading	Plymouth	Redruth	Penzance
① 09 25	09 49	12 36	14 05	14 32
✕① 10 25	10 49	13 51	15 45	16 12
✕① 13 25	13 49	16 33	18 02	18 30
① 16 20F	16 44F	19 54F	21 20F	21 43F
① →	→	20 38	22 04	22 31
✕① 17 25		21 43F	23 12F	23 33F
✕① 18 25F	18 49F	21 43F	23 12F	23 33F
✕① 18 25S	18 49S	22 05S	23 34S	23 55S

F Fridays only
S Saturdays only
For whole or part of the journey
✕ Restaurant service according to time of day
① Hot dishes to order, also drinks and cold snacks

I Hello, there!
J I beg your pardon?
I Hello! How are you getting on?
J Fine, thank you ... sorry ... do I know you?
I Yes, it's me, Nick Fowler!
J Sorry, I don't think I know you.
I Aren't you Harry Shiner?
J Er, no ... I'm afraid not.
I Oh, I'm terribly sorry, I thought you were someone else!

Exercise 3
Listen to the announcements at London–Paddington. Look at the example and complete the chart in the same way.

Number	Train Time	Platform Number	From	To
1	10.25	5	Lon. (London)	Ex. (Exeter St David's)
2				
3				
4				
5				

Exercise 4
How are you?
Very well thanks, and you?
1 Hi!
2 Good afternoon.
3 I'm very sorry.
4 Thank you very much for helping me.
5 How do you do?
6 Aren't you Elton John?
7 How are you getting on?
8 Excuse me.
9 Here you are.
10 Goodbye!

IS EVERYTHING READY?

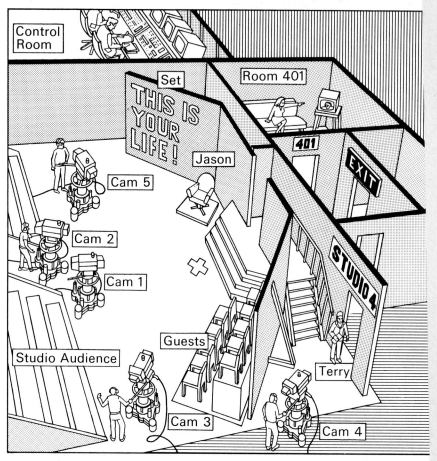

Northern T.V.

Programme	This is Your Life
Date	3rd Nov.
Studio	4
Subject	Jason Douglas
Compere	Terry Donovan
Director	Chris Price

Running order

Pre-show

7.00 Admit studio audience.
7.30 'Warm-up' (Comedian tells jokes to studio audience.)
7.55 Studio car arrives. (7 minute walk to studio.)

Show

8.00 Start videotape, titles & music.
8.01 Terry introduces show.
8.02 Jason arrives. Terry greets him.

Guests

8.03 Jason's sister from Australia.
8.05 His schoolteacher.
8.08 Maria Montrose, actress.
8.10 Father
8.13 Mother
8.15 Charles Orson, film director.
8.18 His first girlfriend.
8.20 Steve Newman, actor (his best friend).
8.22 Norma Phillips, film critic.
8.25-8.28 Show videotape extract from Jason's latest film.
8.29 His brothers and sisters.
8.30 Show ends. Start videotape, credits and music.

Post-show

8.30-8.45 Studio audience leaves.
8.45 Champagne party for Jason and guests.

'This is Your Life' is one of the most popular programmes on British and American television. Every week a famous person is invited to a television studio, without knowing that he or she will be the subject of the programme. The compère meets the person outside the studio and says 'This is your life!'. The person then meets friends and relatives from his or her past and present. Studio 4 is where the programme is recorded. The programme begins at eight o'clock. It's 6.45 now and the director is checking the preparations with his new production assistant. The subject of tonight's show will be an actor, Jason Douglas. The compère, as usual, will be Terry Donovan.

Director Let's just check the arrangements. We're bringing Jason Douglas here in a studio car – he thinks he's coming to a discussion programme! The driver has been told to arrive at exactly 7.55. Now, the programme begins at eight o'clock. At that time Jason will be walking to the studio. Terry Donovan will start his introduction at 8.01, and Jason will arrive at 8.02. Terry will meet him at the studio entrance ... Camera 4 will be there. Then he'll take him to that seat. It'll be on Camera 3. Jason will be sitting there during the whole programme. For most of the show Terry will be standing in the middle, and he'll be on Camera 2. The guests will come through that door, talk to Terry and Jason ... and then sit over there.

Director Now, is that all clear?
Production Assistant Yes ... there's just one thing.
Director Well, what is it?
PA Who's going to look after the guests during the show?
Director Pauline is.
PA And where will they be waiting during the show?
Director In Room 401, as usual. Pauline will be waiting with them, and she'll be watching the show on the monitor. She'll tell them two minutes before they enter.
PA I think that's everything.

Exercise 1
Each of the guests will say a few words about Jason.
A *Who'll be speaking at 8.06?*
B *His schoolteacher will.*
Ask and answer about: 8.04, 8.10, 8.16, 8.19, 8.23.

Exercise 2
A *What'll be happening at 7.45?*
B *A comedian will be telling jokes to the audience.*
Ask and answer about: 7.57, 8.35 and 9.00.

Exercise 3
The guests will be waiting in Room 401 from 7.50 until they enter.
A *How long will his sister be waiting?*
B *She'll be waiting for thirteen minutes.*
Ask and answer about the other guests.

THIS IS YOUR LIFE!

Terry Good evening and welcome to 'This is Your Life'. This is Terry Donovan speaking. We're waiting for the subject of tonight's programme. He's one of the world's leading actors, and he thinks he's coming here to take part in a discussion programme ... I can hear him now ... yes, here he is! Jason Douglas ... This is your life!

Jason Oh, no ... I don't believe it! Not me ...

Terry Yes, you! Now come over here and sit down. Jason, you were born at number 28 Balaclava Street in East Ham, London on July 2nd 1947. You were one of six children, and your father was a taxi driver. Of course, your name was then Graham Smith.

Terry Now, do you know this voice? 'I remember Jason when he was two. He used to scream and shout all day.'

Jason Susan!

Terry Yes ... all the way from Sydney, Australia ... she flew here specially for this programme. It's your sister, Susan Fraser!

Jason Susan ... why didn't you tell me ... oh, this is wonderful!

Terry Yes, you haven't seen each other for 13 years ... take a seat next to him, Susan. You started school at the age of five, in 1952, and in 1958 you moved to Lane End Secondary School.

Terry Do you remember this voice? 'Smith! Stop looking out of the window!'

Jason Oh, no! It's Mr Hooper!

Terry Your English teacher, Mr Stanley Hooper. Was Jason a good student, Mr Hooper?

Mr Hooper Eh? No, he was the worst in the class ... but he was a brilliant actor, even in those days. He could imitate all the teachers!

Terry Thank you, Mr Hooper. You can speak to Jason, later. Well, you went to the London School of Drama in 1966, and left in 1969. In 1973 you went to Hollywood.

Terry Do you know this voice?. 'Hi Jason ... Can you ride a horse yet?'

Jason Maria!

Terry Maria Montrose ... who's come from Hollywood to be with you tonight.

Maria Hello, Jason ... it's great to be here. Hello, Terry. Jason and I were in a movie together in 1974. Jason had to learn to ride a horse ... well, Jason doesn't like horses very much.

Jason Like them! I'm terrified of them!

Maria Anyway, he practised for two weeks. Then he went to the director

... it was Charles Orson ... and said, 'What do you want me to do?' Charles said, 'I want you to fall off the horse'. Jason was furious. He said, 'What? Fall off! I've been practising for two weeks ... I could fall off the first day ... without any practice!'

Look at this

Northern T.V.	
Programme:	This is your life
Date:	3rd. November
Studio:	4
Subject:	Jason Douglas
Compère:	Terry Donovan
Director:	Chris Price
Surname:	Smith
First name(s):	Graham Anthony
(stage name:	Jason Douglas)
Date of birth:	2/7/47
Nationality:	British
Place of birth:	London, England
Education:	Lane End Secondary 1958-65 London School of Drama 1966-69
Address:	3280 Sunshine Boulevard, Hollywood, California.
Marital status:	Single
Profession:	Actor

Northern T.V.	
Programme:	
Date:	
Studio:	
Subject:	
Compère:	
Director:	
Surname:	
First name(s):	
Date of birth:	
Nationality:	
Place of birth:	
Education:	
Address:	
Marital status:	
Profession:	

Ask questions, and complete the form for another student.

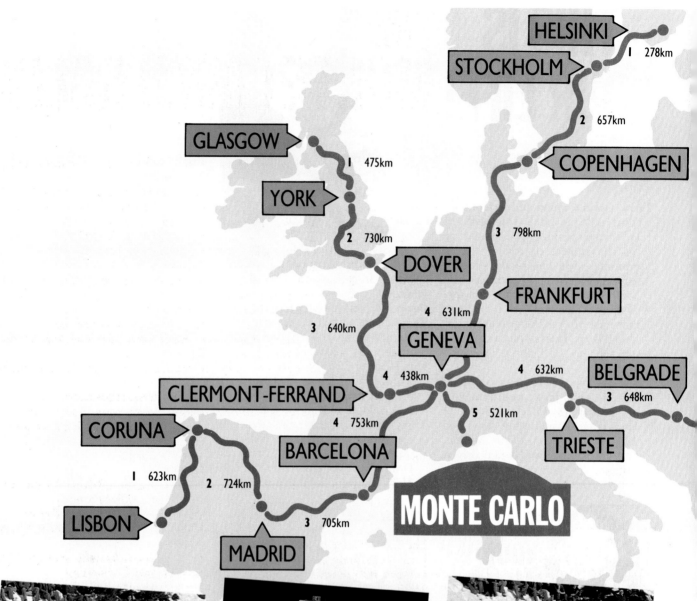

HELSINKI

STOCKHOLM

1 278km

2 657km

GLASGOW

COPENHAGEN

1 475km

YORK

3 798km

2 730km

DOVER

FRANKFURT

4 631km

3 640km

GENEVA

CLERMONT-FERRAND

4 632km

BELGRADE

4 438km

3 648km

CORUNA

5 521km

TRIESTE

BARCELONA

4 753km

1 623km

2 724km

LISBON

3 705km

MADRID

MONTE CARLO

Driver Russell Cook
Nationality British   *Age* 28
Starting point Glasgow
Car Talbot Sunbeam Lotus
Engine capacity 2172 cc
Maximum speed 196 km/h
Petrol consumption:
urban cycle 15.59 litres/100 km
constant 90 km/h 13.1 litres/100 km
Length 3.82 m
Width 1.60 m
Height 1.39 m

Driver Hannu Larsen
Nationality Finnish   *Age* 32
Starting point Helsinki
Car Audi Quattro
Engine capacity 2144 cc
Maximum speed 220 km/h
Petrol consumption:
urban cycle 15.69 litres/100 km
constant 90 km/h 7.91 litres/100 km
Length 4.40 m
Width 1.72 m
Height 1.34 m

Driver Danielle Bernard
Nationality French   *Age* 31
Starting point Lisbon
Car Renault 5 Gordini
Engine capacity 1397 cc
Maximum speed 176 km/h
Petrol consumption:
urban cycle 11.2 litres/100 km
constant 90 km/h 6.1 litres/100 km
Length 3.50 m
Width 1.52 m
Height 1.39 m

Start

Sunday

Monday

Tuesday

Wednesday

Thursday

THE MONTE CARLO RALLY

2 703km

THESSALONIKI

1 543km

ATHENS

Driver Sandro Rossi
Nationality Italian   *Age* 30
Starting point Athens
Car Fiat 131
Engine capacity 1585 cc
Maximum speed 168 km/h
Petrol consumption:
urban cycle 11.92 litres/100 km
constant 90 km/h 6.99 litres/100 km
Length 4.26 m
Width 1.65 m
Height 1.39 m

The Monte Carlo Rally, which started in 1911, is Europe's most famous motoring event. Competitors leave from several points around Europe and follow routes of approximately equal length to a rallying point which will be Geneva this year. They then follow a single route to the finish. The rally consists of five daily stages, beginning on Sunday morning, and each competitor will have driven about 3000 kilometres by Thursday night. It is not a race. The winner is decided on a points system. Drivers have to maintain an average speed between control points, and there are also special tests of driving skill in different conditions on the way.

Motoring news

This is Radio Wessex on 203 metres, medium wave. It's nine o'clock on Monday 25th January and this is Barry King reporting from Dover. The British competitors in the Monte Carlo Rally have just arrived here at the end of the second stage in this year's competition. Russell Cook, who's driving a Sunbeam Lotus, is leading. The Triumph driven by Tony Bond, who won last year's rally, crashed in Yorkshire this morning. Tony was unhurt but will be unable to continue. Seven other cars have withdrawn due to bad weather conditions. Tonight the cars, which left from Glasgow on Sunday morning, will be crossing the English Channel.

Exercise 1
Look at the first driver.
What's his name?
His name's Russell Cook.
Where does he come from?
He comes from Britain
How old is he? He's 28.
Ask and answer about the other drivers.

Exercise 2
Look at the first car. (All statistics are for production cars.)
What make is it? It's a Sunbeam Lotus.

How fast can it go? The top speed is 196 km/h.
How much petrol does it use? 15.59 litres per 100 km around town, and 13.1 litres at a constant 90 km/h.
How long is it? 3.82 m.
How wide is it? 1.60 m.
How high is it? 1.39 m.
Ask and answer about the other cars.

Exercise 3
Look at the drivers and the cars.
Danielle Bernard's older than Sandro Rossi.
Russell Cook isn't as old as Danielle Bernard.
Hannu Larsen's the oldest.
Make comparisons about the cars using: fast/long/wide/high/economical.

Exercise 4
Look at the first driver. All the cars started on Sunday morning.
Where is he now? He's in Dover.
Where did he start? He started from Glasgow.
How long has he been driving? He's been driving for two days.
How many kilometres has he driven? 1205 km.
Ask and answer about the other drivers.

Exercise 5
Look at the first driver. It's Monday night.
Where will he be tomorrow night? He'll be in Clermont-Ferrand.
What will he be doing tomorrow? He'll be driving from Dover to Clermont-Ferrand.
Ask and answer about Wednesday and Thursday.
Do the same for the other drivers.

Exercise 6
Look at the first driver.
On Tuesday night he'll be in Clermont-Ferrand.
How far will he have driven on Tuesday? He'll have driven 640 km.
Ask and answer about Wednesday and Thursday.
Do the same for the other drivers.

Unit 4

OUT OF WORK

In Britain a lot of people are out of work. Tracey Chapman is 18, and she left school a year ago. She lives in the North East, an area of high youth unemployment. She hasn't been able to find a job yet.

'My dad just doesn't understand. He started working in a steel mill when he was 15. Things are different now, but he thinks I should start bringing home some money. Oh, I get my unemployment benefit, but that isn't much and I'm fed up with queuing for it every Thursday. I hate having to ask my mum and dad for money. Oh, my mum gives me a couple of pounds for tights now and then, but she can't stand seeing me at home all day. I've almost given up looking for a job. I buy the local paper every day but I'm really tired of looking through the "Situations Vacant" column. There are 50 applicants for every job. I was interested in being a dentist's receptionist because I like meeting people, but now I'd take any job at all. People ask me why I don't move to London, but I don't want to leave my family and friends. Anyway, I'm scared of living on my own in a big city.'

Tracey Chapman went to the Careers Advisory Service. She had to complete this questionnaire.

QUESTIONNAIRE

1 Are you seeking
a full-time employment? ☐
b part-time employment? ☐

2 Which of these is most important for you?
(Please number 1 – 5 in order of importance.)
money ☐   people ☐   security ☐
job satisfaction ☐   an interesting job ☐

3 Do you like   yes   no
a meeting people?   ☐   ☐
b working alone?   ☐   ☐
c working with other people?   ☐   ☐
d working with your hands?   ☐   ☐
e travelling?   ☐   ☐

4 What do you like doing in your free time?

George Morley is 54. Until last year he was a production manager in the textile industry. He had worked for the same company since he left school. He had a good job, a four-bedroomed house and a company car. When his company had to close because of economic difficulties, he became redundant.

'It's funny really ... I don't feel old, but it isn't easy to start looking for a job at my age. I've had so many refusals. Now I'm frightened of applying for a job. All the interviewers are twenty years younger than me. You see, I'm interested in learning a new skill, but nobody wants to train me. I can see their point of view. I'll have to retire in ten years. It's just ... well, I'm tired of sitting around the house. I've worked hard for nearly forty years and now I'm terrified of having nothing to do. When I was still with Lancastrian Textiles I was bored with doing the same thing day after day, but now I'd really enjoy doing a job again ... any job really. It's not the money ... I got good redundancy pay, and the house is paid for ... and I've given up smoking ... no, it's not just money. I just need to feel ... well, useful ... that's all.'

Exercise 1
I like meeting people.
Make sentences about yourself with:
love/enjoy/don't like/dislike/hate/can't stand.

Exercise 2
I'm scared of living on my own.
Make sentences about yourself with:
afraid of/frightened of/terrified of.

Exercise 3
I'm bored with doing the same thing.
Make sentences about yourself with:
fed up with/tired of/interested in.

Exercise 4
I gave up smoking.
Make sentences about yourself with:
start/begin/stop/give up.

GETTING A JOB

In Britain there is a special service for school leavers, The Careers Advisory Service, which helps young people who are looking for their first jobs. Careers Officers give practical advice on interview techniques, application forms, letters, pay, National Insurance and Trade Unions. This is an extract from a leaflet which is given to young people by Dorset Careers Service.

THE INTERVIEW

You've got an interview for a job – good! So now for the hard work. To do well at an interview you need to put in some thought first.

The employer wants to know if you are the person he wants, so you'll be asked about yourself. Think about it now:

What do I do well?	School activities?
What are my good points?	School subjects?
Why would I like this job?	Previous work?
Spare-time interests?	Saturday job?
What is my family like?	

What do I like doing and why?
What do I not like doing and why?

You will want to ask questions too.

The job itself?	Can I see where I
Training?	would be working?
Prospects?	Hours?
Further Education?	£ £ £ ?
Conditions?	

Write your questions down and take them with you.

BEFORE THE INTERVIEW

1 Find out what you can about the firm.
2 Find out the interviewer's name and telephone number.
3 Find out where the interview is.
4 Find out how long it will take to get there.
5 Make sure you know what the job involves.
6 Dress to look clean and tidy.

AT THE INTERVIEW

1 Do arrive early. Phone if you're held up.
2 Do try to smile.
3 Do show interest in the job and ask questions.
4 Do be polite.
5 Don't panic, even if faced by more than one person.
6 Don't slouch around and look bored.
7 Don't smoke or chew.
8 Don't give one word answers or say you don't care what you do.

Look at these job advertisements.

Trainee computer programmer
Good opportunity for a start in computers. Ability at maths is essential. Application forms from: Personnel Department, Continental Computers, Honeywell Rd., Bournemouth.

Fernside Engineering
Require a junior clerk for the accounts department.
Apply in writing to: The Personnel Officer, Fernside Engineering, Western Rd., Poole.

Shop assistant
A vacancy for a smart, lively young person. Good prospects. Please write to:
Mrs J.. Frost, 'Cool Boutique', 39 High St., Dorchester.

Applying by letter
1 Remember that first impressions are important.
2 Write clearly and neatly on good notepaper, unlined if possible.
3 Check for spelling mistakes. Use a dictionary if you are not sure of a word.
4 Describe yourself, your qualifications and your experience clearly.
5 If the advertisement asks you to write for an application form you will not need to give detailed information in your letter.
6 Address the letter and the envelope clearly.

44 Deepdale Road,
Boscombe,
Bournemouth,
BH92 7JX

4th April, 1982

The Personnel Department,
Continental Computers,
Honeywell Road,
Bournemouth

Dear Sir or Madam,
I read your advertisement in yesterday's 'Evening Echo'. I am interested in training as a computer programmer. Could you please send me an application form, and any further details.

Yours faithfully,

Joanne Evans

BATTLE OF TRAFALGAR STREET

Last night, for the third time this week, police and County Council officials had to turn and run when they were showered with boiling water from the upstairs window of No 10 Trafalgar Street. They were hoping to speak to Mrs Florence Hamilton, an 83-year-old widow, who is still refusing to leave her home. Every other house in the street has been demolished. The Council are planning to build four 20-storey blocks of flats in the area. All the other residents agreed to move when the Council offered to provide them with new flats nearby. On Tuesday evening a social worker who wanted to speak to Mrs Hamilton was attacked and badly bitten by one of her dogs.

Radio report 1

This is Pennine Radio News, Alan Nelson reporting from Trafalgar Street. Mr Hardy, the Tadworth Housing Officer, has agreed to speak to us.

Alan Now, Mr Hardy, has the situation changed since last night?

Hardy No, it hasn't. Mrs Hamilton is still there, and she's still refusing to talk to us.

Alan Well, what are you going to do?

Hardy It's a very difficult situation. We'd like her to come out peacefully. The police don't intend to prosecute her ... but she's a very stubborn lady!

Alan Stubborn? Yes, well, it is her home.

Hardy I agree, and it's been her home for a long time, I know. But nobody else refused to move. You see, a lot of people in this area are living in sub-standard accommodation and we are going to build over 300 flats on this site. Families are expecting to move into them next year! It's all being delayed because of one person!

Alan But Mrs Hamilton was born in that house.

Hardy Of course, of course. But we have promised to give her a modern flat immediately, a very nice flat which is ideal for an elderly person living alone.

Alan So, what happens next?

Hardy I don't know. I really don't ... but we can't wait forever. The police will have to do something soon. It won't be easy. She's got two very big dogs, and they don't like strangers!

Radio report 2

We have also managed to arrange an interview with Mrs Hamilton. She has decided to speak to us but she has demanded to see me alone.

Mrs Hamilton!

Mrs H. Who are you?

Alan I'm Alan Nelson ... Pennine Radio News.

Mrs H. Well ... don't come any closer, or I'll let the dogs out. Down Caesar! Sit, boy!

Alan I'm sure our listeners would like to hear your side of the story.

Mrs H. There's not much to say. I'm not moving! I was born here, I had my children here, and I intend to die here.

Alan But the Council really need to have this land, and they have arranged to provide a new flat for you ...

Mrs H. Oh, yes. I know, but I can't take my dogs with me ... and I need to have company. My dogs are all I've got. Down boy!

Alan How long can you stay here?

Mrs H. Oh, I've got plenty of food. The Council have threatened to cut off the water and electricity, but I'll be all right.

Alan Well, thank you, Mrs Hamilton ... and good luck!

Mrs H. And you can tell the Council from me ... I want another house where I can keep my dogs, not a little flat in a bloody high-rise block!

Exercise

'... a Social Worker who **wanted to speak** to Mrs Hamilton ...' 'wanted to speak' is 'verb + to (do)'.

Go through the page and underline the other examples of verbs with 'to (do)'.

SENDING A CARD

Greetings cards are big business in Britain. Millions of cards are sent every year, and you can buy cards for nearly every special occasion. There are cards for Christmas, New Year, Easter, birthdays, engagements, funerals, St Valentine's day, Mother's Day, Father's Day, retirement, illness, passing examinations and driving tests, promotions, and the picture postcards sent by holidaymakers. ·

TWINS! How Wonderful!!

To Linda & David,
We were delighted to hear about the twins! It's lovely to have two at the same time... double the happiness (and double the work!) We're willing to help at any time. Don't hesitate to ask.
Lots of love,
Alison & Kevin

Best Wishes for Your 21st Birthday

You've never been 21 before,
Now you've got the key of the door,
It's really great to be 21,
Now you are a man, my son.
Love, Dad

Christine

Best Wishes on your Wedding

It was very nice to read about your wedding. I expect your parents are sorry to lose a daughter but happy to gain a son! My best wishes to you and your new husband.
Sarah Roberts

To Harold and Enid,

Congratulations on your Silver Wedding

Twenty five years together! I was really surprised to hear it. You don't look old enough to have a silver wedding! Very best wishes,
Gladys.

With
Sincere
Sympathy

I was very sad to learn about Albert's death. It is difficult to know what to say. As you know, I worked with him for thirty years. He was a wonderful person... He was always ready to help everyone. He will be sadly missed. I am sorry, but I was too ill to come to the funeral. Yours sincerely
Walter Brown

25

Get Well Soon

I was very upset to hear about your accident. I enclose some magazines. You'll need something interesting to look at! I hope the nurses are nice.
All the best.
Freddie

Wedding anniversaries
The traditional gifts to give for each one:

1st paper	13th lace
2nd cotton	14th ivory
3rd leather	15th glass
4th linen	20th china
5th wood	**25th silver**
6th iron	30th pearl
7th wool	35th jade
8th bronze	40th ruby
9th pottery	45th sapphire
10th tin	**50th gold**
11th steel	55th emerald
12th silk	**60th diamond**

Exercise
Can you suggest a suitable gift for each anniversary?
2nd anniversary
A cotton table-cloth or some cotton towels

Unit 8

MARRIAGE GUIDANCE COUNCIL

Malcolm and Barbara Harris have been married for nearly fifteen years. They've got two children, Gary aged thirteen, and Andrea, who is eleven. During the last couple of years Malcolm and Barbara haven't been very happy. They argue all the time. Barbara's sister advised them to go to the Marriage Guidance Council. There is one in most British towns. It's an organization which allows people to talk with a third person about their problems. This is their third visit, and Mrs Murray, the counsellor, always sees them.

Barbara's interview

Mrs Murray Ah, come in Barbara. Take a seat. Is your husband here?

Barbara Yes, he's waiting outside. He didn't want to come here this week, but ... well, I persuaded him to come.

Mrs Murray I see. How have things been?

Barbara Oh, much the same. We still seem to have rows all the time.

Mrs Murray What do you quarrel about?

Barbara What don't we quarrel about, you mean! Oh, everything. You see, he's so inconsiderate ...

Mrs Murray Go on.

Barbara Well, I'll give you an example. You know, when the children started school, I wanted to go back to work again, too. So I got a job. Well, anyway, by the time I've collected Gary and Andrea from school, I only get home about half an hour before Malcom ...

Mrs Murray Yes?

Barbara Well, when he gets home, he expects me to run around and get his tea. He never does anything in the house!

Mrs Murray Mmm.

Barbara And last Friday! He invited three of his friends to come round for a drink. He didn't tell me to expect them, and I'd had a long and difficult day. I don't think that's right, do you?

Mrs Murray Barbara, I'm not here to pass judgement. I'm here to listen.

Barbara Sorry. And he's so untidy. He's worse than the kids. I always have to remind him to pick up his clothes. He just throws them on the floor. After all, I'm not his servant. I've got my own career. Actually, I think that's part of the trouble. You see, I earn as much money as he does.

Malcolm's interview

Mrs Murray Malcolm! I'm so glad you could come.

Malcolm Hello, Mrs Murray. Well, I'll be honest. Barbara had to force me to come, really.

Mrs Murray Does it embarrass you to talk about your problems?

Malcolm Yes, it does. But I suppose we need to talk to somebody.

Mrs Murray Barbara feels that you ... well, you resent her job.

Malcolm I don't know. I would prefer her to stay at home, but she's very well qualified... and I encouraged her to go back to work. Now the kids are at school, she needs an interest ... and I suppose we need the money.

Mrs Murray How do you share the housework?

Malcom I try to help. I always help her to wash up, and I help Gary and Andrea to do their homework while she does the dinner. But she doesn't think that's enough. What do you think?

Mrs Murray I'm not here to give an opinion, Malcolm.

Malcolm I think we're both too tired, that's all. In the evenings we're both too tired to talk. And Barbara ... she never allows me to suggest anything about the house or about the kids. We always have the same arguments. She's got her own opinions and that's it. Last night we had another row. She's forbidden the kids to ride their bikes to school.

Mrs Murray Why?

Malcolm She thinks they're too young to ride in the traffic. But I think they should. She always complains about collecting them from school. But you can't wrap children in cotton-wool, can you?

Exercise 1

'Barbara's sister advised *them* to go ...'

There are fifteen sentences like this. Underline them or write them out.

Exercise 2

They're very tired. They can't talk.
They're too tired to talk.
Continue.

1 They're very young. They shouldn't ride to school.
2 He's very old. He can't go to work.
3 We were very surprised. We couldn't say anything.
4 She's very ill. She shouldn't go out.

A FUNNY THING HAPPENED TO ME...

A funny thing happened to me last Friday. I'd gone to London to do some shopping. I wanted to get some Christmas presents, and I needed to find some books for my course at college (you see, I'm a student). I caught an early train to London, so by early afternoon I'd bought everything that I wanted. Anyway, I'm not very fond of London, all the noise and traffic, and I'd made some arrangements for that evening. So, I took a taxi to Waterloo station. I can't really afford taxis, but I wanted to get the 3.30 train. Unfortunately the taxi got stuck in a traffic jam, and by the time I got to Waterloo, the train had just gone. I had to wait an hour for the next one. I bought an evening newspaper, the 'Standard', and wandered over to the station buffet. At that time of day it's nearly empty, so I bought a coffee and a packet of biscuits ... chocolate biscuits. I'm very fond of chocolate biscuits. There were plenty of empty tables and I found one near the window. I sat down and began doing the crossword. I always enjoy doing crossword puzzles.

After a couple of minutes a man sat down opposite me. There was nothing special about him, except that he was very tall. In fact he looked like a typical city businessman ... you know, dark suit and briefcase. I didn't say anything and I carried on with my crossword. Suddenly he reached across the table, opened my packet of biscuits, took one, dipped it into his coffee and popped it into his mouth. I couldn't believe my eyes! I was too shocked to say anything. Anyway, I didn't want to make a fuss, so I decided to ignore it. I always avoid trouble if I can. I just took a biscuit myself and went back to my crossword.

When the man took a second biscuit, I didn't look up and I didn't make a sound. I pretended to be very interested in the puzzle. After a couple of minutes, I casually put out my hand, took the last biscuit and glanced at the man. He was staring at me furiously. I nervously put the biscuit in my mouth, and decided to leave. I was ready to get up and go when the man suddenly pushed back his chair, stood up and hurried out of the buffet. I felt very relieved and decided to wait two or three minutes before going myself. I finished my coffee, folded my newspaper and stood up. And there, on the table, where my newspaper had been, was my packet of biscuits.

Exercise

I always do my homework.
We have to do military service in my country.
I never make a fuss.
I made my bed this morning.
Write ten sentences, five with 'do' and five with 'make'.

Look at this:

'I'd gone to London to *do* some shopping.'
'I always enjoy *doing* crossword puzzles.'
'I'd *made* some arrangements.'
'I didn't want to *make* a fuss.'
'I didn't *make* a sound.'

Do	Make
shopping	arrangements
work	an offer
homework	a suggestion
housework	a decision
cleaning	an attempt
washing up	an effort
gardening	an excuse
military service	a mistake
mathematics,	a noise
history,	a phonecall
literature, etc.	a date
(at school)	a profit
something	a bed
interesting	a cake
a (boring) job	a speech
	trouble

POLITE REQUESTS

Max Millwall used to be a popular comedian on British radio. He's nearly 70 now, but he still performs in clubs in the Midlands and North of England. He's on stage now at the All-Star Variety Club in Wigan.

Well, good evening, ladies and gentlemen ... and others! It's nice to be back in Wigan again. Well, I have to say that, I say it every night. I said it last night. The only trouble was that I was in Birmingham. I thought the audience looked confused! Actually, I remember Wigan very well indeed. Really! You know, the first time I came here was in the 1930s. I was very young and very shy ... thank you, mother. No, you can't believe that, can you? Well, it's true. I was very young and very shy. Anyway, the first Saturday night I was in Wigan, I decided to go to the local dance-hall. Do you remember the old 'Majestic Ballroom' in Wythenshawe Street? There's a multi-storey car park there now. It was a lovely place ... always full of beautiful girls, (the ballroom, not the car park). Of course, most of them are grandmothers now! Oh, you were there too, were you, love? I was much too shy to ask anyone for a dance. So I sat down at a table, and I

thought I'd watch for a while. You know, see how the other lads did it. At the next table there was a lovely girl in a blue dress. She'd arrived with a friend, but her friend was dancing with someone. This bloke came over to her, he was very posh, wearing a dinner-jacket and a bow tie! Well, he walked up to her and said, 'Excuse me, may I have the pleasure of the next dance?' She looked up at him (she had lovely big blue eyes) and said 'Eh? What did you say?' So he said, 'I wonder if you would be kind enough to dance with me ... er ... if you don't mind.' 'Eee ... no, thank you very much,' she replied.

A few minutes later, this other chap arrived. He had a blue suit, a nice tie, and a little moustache. He gave her this big smile, and said, 'Would you be so kind as to have the next dance with me?' 'Pardon?' she said. I thought to myself 'She's a bit deaf ... or maybe she hasn't washed her ears recently.'

'Would you mind having the next dance with me?' he said, a bit nervously this time. 'Eee, no thanks, love. I'm finishing my lemonade,' she replied. 'Blimey! I thought. This looks a bit difficult.'

Then this third fellow came over. He was very good-looking, you know, black teeth, white hair ... sorry, I mean white teeth, black hair! 'May I ask you something?' he said, ever so politely. 'If you like,' she answered. 'Can I ... I mean ... could I ... no, might I have the next dance with you?' 'Oooh, sorry,' she said. 'My feet are aching. I've been standing up all day at the shop.'

By now, I was terrified. I mean, she'd said 'no' to all of them! Then this fourth character thought he'd try.

'Would you like to dance?' he said. 'What?' she replied. She was a lovely girl, but I didn't think much of her voice! 'Do you want to dance?' he said. She looked straight at him. 'No', she said. That's all. 'No.' Well, I decided to go home. I was wearing an old jacket and trousers, and nobody would say that I was good-looking! Just as I was walking past her table, she smiled. 'Er ... dance?' I said. 'Thank you very much,' she replied. And that was that! It's our fortieth wedding anniversary next week.

Exercise 1
Go through and underline all the 'requests'. How many are there?

Exercise 2
There are six words that mean 'man'. What are they?

Exercise 3
Find expressions that mean:
1 smart and upper class
2 with several floors
3 unable to hear well
4 handsome
5 a short time

A Mike ...
B Yes?
A Shut the door will you? It's freezing in here!
B Right ... sorry.

close window/cold
open door/very hot

C Karen ...
D Yes?
C Lend me 20p. I've left my purse in the office.
D Oh, OK. Here you are.
C Thanks.

£1/wallet   50p/handbag

E Excuse me, could you pass me the sugar?
F Oh, yes. Of course. There you are.
E Thank you very much.

vinegar   salt   pepper

G Can I help you?
H Oh, thank you. Would you mind putting my case on the rack?
G Not at all. There you are.
H Oh, thank you so much. You're very kind.

luggage/up there   bags/rack

I Excuse me. It's a bit stuffy in here. Do you mind if I open the window?
J No, no. I don't mind at all. I feel like some fresh air too.

cold/close/cold too
feels hot/stuffy too

K Excuse me, Mrs Howe. May I ask you something?
L Yes, Wendy, What is it?
K May I have the day off next Friday?
L Well, we're very busy. Is it important?
K Er, yes, it is, really. It's my cousin's wedding.
L Oh, well! Of course you can.

Tuesday Wednesday Thursday
cousin brother nephew niece

M Can I help you, sir?
N I beg your pardon?
M Can I help you, sir?
N Oh, no ... no, thank you. I'm just looking.

madam miss
pardon? sorry?

O Good morning.
P Good morning. I wonder if you can help me. I'm trying to find a Christmas present, for my father.
O Might I suggest a tie?
P Hmm ... perhaps. Could you show me some ties?

wedding/cousin/some towels
birthday/sister/scarf

Q Excuse me ...
R Yes?
Q I wonder if you'd be kind enough to get me one of those tins ... on the top shelf. I can't reach it.
R Certainly. There you are.
Q Thank you very much indeed.

packet jar box bottle

A TRIP TO SPAIN

Norman Garrard is a trainee sales representative. He's 22, and he works for a company that sells toys. He's going to Spain on business. It's his first business trip abroad, and he's packing his suitcase. He lives with his parents, and his mother is helping him, and fussing.

Mrs Garrard Norman ... haven't you finished packing yet?
Norman No, Mum. But it's all right. There isn't much to do.
Mrs Garrard Well, I'll give you a hand. Oh, there isn't much room left. Is there anywhere to put your toilet bag?
Norman Yes, yes ... it'll go in here. Now, I've got three more shirts to pack ... they'll go on top ... but there's another pair of shoes to get in. I don't know where to put them.
Mrs Garrard Put them down the side. Right. I think we can close it now.

Norman Right. Where's the label?
Mrs Garrard Which label, dear?
Norman The airline label to put on the suitcase. Ah, here it is.
Mrs Garrard Now, have you got the key?
Norman Which key?
Mrs Garrard The key to lock the case, of course.
Norman It's in the lock, Mum. Don't fuss. There's nothing to worry about. There's plenty of time.
Mrs Garrard Have you forgotten anything?
Norman I hope not.
Mrs Garrard And you've got a safe pocket to keep your passport in?
Norman Yes, it's in my inside jacket pocket.
Mrs Garrard Have you got a book to read on the plane?
Norman Yes, it's in my briefcase.

Mrs Garrard And has everything been arranged?
Norman What do you mean?
Mrs Garrard Well, is there someone to meet you at the other end?
Norman Oh yes. The Spanish representative's meeting me at the airport.
Mrs Garrard And you've got somewhere to stay tonight?
Norman I hope so! Now, everything's ready. I'll just have to get some pesetas at the airport. I'll need some small change to tip the porter, but that's all.
Mrs Garrard Well, have a good trip, dear ... and look after yourself.
Norman Thanks, Mum.
Mrs Garrard Oh! I nearly forgot! Here are some sweets to suck on the plane, you know, when it's coming down.
Norman Oh. Mum ... don't worry. I'll be all right, really! I'll see you next week.

Exercise 1
Norman lives in Southampton. He went by taxi to the station, then by train to Woking, then by bus to Heathrow and finally by plane to Madrid. How can you get to your nearest international airport? Which is the best way for you?

Exercise 2
Norman made a list. Look at it.
He remembered to pack his shirts.
He forgot to pack his raincoat.
Write seven sentences.

Exercise 3
Imagine that you have just been on a plane. The airline has lost your suitcase. Think about the clothes you would pack for a one week holiday in London, in Spring. Make a list of the clothes you had in your suitcase.
One dark blue woollen pullover.
One brown leather belt.

FLYING TO SPAIN

At the airport

Norman is at Heathrow Airport. He's checked in. He's been through Passport Control and he's in the Departure Lounge. Listen to the announcements. Look at the chart, look at the example, and complete the chart in the same way.

FLIGHT DEPARTURES INFORMATION TIME NOW 11.45				
Carrier	Flight	Time	Destination	Information
British Airways	BA 412	12.00	Amsterdam	Last call Gate 17
S.A.S.				
Iberia				
Alitalia				
Olympic Airways				
Sabena				

In flight

Norman is now on the plane. Listen to the four announcements, and answer these questions.

1. What's the pilot's name?
   How long will the delay be?
   When will they arrive in Madrid?
   What are they waiting for?
2. Where is the plane?
   What kind is it?
   How high is it?
   How fast is it going?
   How hot is it in Madrid?
   What's the weather like?
   Why should the passengers remain in their seats?
3. What's the plane beginning to do?
   What two things should the passengers do?
   When can they start smoking again?
4. What should the passengers do?
   When can they stand up?

EXCUSE ME, YOUNG MAN... WOULD YOU MIND OPENING THE WINDOW? IT'S RATHER HOT IN HERE.

Lunch on the plane

Steward Here's your tray, sir.
Norman Oh, thank you.
Steward Would you like something to drink?
Norman Er ... yes, please. Some red wine.
Steward That's 100 pesetas.
Norman Thanks. Can I pay in British money?
Steward Of course. You needn't pay now, I'll collect it later.

Landing-cards

Steward Spanish national or non-Spanish, sir?
Norman Er ... I'm British.
Steward Would you mind completing this landing card, sir?
Norman Right. Thank you.

Landing-card

Family name...... GARRARD.............
Forename(s) .. NORMAN..IAN..........
Father's name .DUNCAN. ALISTAIR.
Place of birth... WINCHESTER.........
Nationality .... BRITISH.................
Passport no .... N.1054.372...........
Permanent address. 37.CUNARD.AVENUE,
.... SOUTHAMPTON, ENGLAND...
Point of departure .LONDON.(HEATHROW)
Destination .... MADRID.............
Date 14..4.83 Signature N.I.Garrard......

Passport control

Official Passport, please. Thank you. Where have you come from, sir?
Norman London.
Official And what's the purpose of your visit ... business or pleasure?
Norman Business.
Official Fine ... and how long will you be staying here?
Norman Just for five days.
Official Thank you, Mr Garrard. I hope you enjoy your visit.

MONEY

Money is used for buying or selling goods, for measuring value and for storing wealth. Almost every society now has a money economy based on coins and paper notes of one kind or another. However, this has not always been true. In primitive societies a system of barter was used. Barter was a system of direct exchange of goods. Somebody could exchange a sheep, for example, for anything in the market-place that they considered to be of equal value. Bárter, however, was a very unsatisfactory system because people's precise needs seldom coincided. People needed a more practical system of exchange, and various money systems developed based on goods which the members of a society recognized as having value. Cattle, grain, teeth, shells, feathers, skulls, salt, elephant tusks and tobacco have all been used. Precious metals gradually took over because, when made into coins, they were portable, durable, recognizable and divisible into larger and smaller units of value.

A coin is a piece of metal, usually disc-shaped, which bears lettering, designs or numbers showing its value. Until the eighteenth and nineteenth centuries coins were given monetary worth based on the exact amount of metal contained in them, but most modern coins are based on face value, the value that governments choose to give them, irrespective of the actual metal content. Coins have been made of gold (Au), silver (Ag), copper (Cu), aluminium (Al), nickel (Ni), lead (Pb), zinc (Zn), plastic, and in China even from pressed tea leaves. Most governments now issue paper money in the form of notes, which are really 'promises to pay'. Paper money is obviously easier to handle and much more convenient in the modern world. Cheques, bankers' cards, and credit cards are being used increasingly and it is possible to imagine a world where 'money' in the form of coins and paper currency will no longer be used. Even today, in the United States, many places – especially filling stations – will not accept cash at night for security reasons.

Exercise 1
Find expressions which mean:
1 A place to buy petrol.
2 A place where goods are bought and sold.
3 The period between 1801 and 1900.
4 The bony structure of the head.
5 Round and flat in shape.
6 An exchange of goods for other goods.

Exercise 2
Find words which mean:
1 Can be divided.
2 Lasts a long time.
3 Can be carried.
4 Can be recognized.

Exercise 3
Put these words in the correct places in the sentences below:
coins/cash/currency/money.
1 The...of Japan is the yen.
2 She has got a lot of ... in her bank account.
3 It costs £10 if you're paying .... It'll be more if you pay by cheque.
4 Can you change this pound note into ... for the coffee machine?

Exercise 4
Money is used for buying goods
means: .You can buy goods with it.
Write similar sentences which mean:
1 You can measure value with it.
2 You can store wealth with it.
3 You can sell things for it.

Exercise 5
Money is used for buying and selling goods.
People use money for buying and selling goods.
Change these sentences in the same way.
1 A system of barter was used.
2 Cattle, grain and tobacco have all been used.
3 Paper currency will no longer be used.
4 Cheques, bankers' cards and credit cards are being used.

Exercise 6
Somebody could exchange a sheep.
A sheep could be exchanged.
Change these sentences in the same way.
1 People needed a more practical system.
2 Most governments now issue paper money in the form of notes.
3 Filling stations will not accept cash at night.

Exercise 7
Money *is used for buying things.*
Shampoo *is used for washing your hair.*
Make sentences with: knife/pen/key/camera/suitcase/saucepan/toothpaste/detergent/wallet/hair-dryer.

Exercise 8
A place where you can fill your petrol tank is a *filling station.*
Complete these sentences.
1 A special room where you can wait is a ....
2 A pill which helps you to sleep is a ....
3 A licence which allows you to drive is a ....
4 A glove which boxers wear is a ....
5 Oil you can cook with is ....
6 A pool where you can swim is a ....
7 Special liquid you can wash up with is ....
8 A boat with sails is a ....

MONEY, MONEY, MONEY

Bargaining

Lucy is in the Portobello Road street market in London. She's looking at an antique stall, and she's just seen a brass plate. She collects brass ornaments and she's interested in buying it. Listen to her conversation with the stall-holder, and answer these questions.

1 How much does he say it's worth?
2 How much is he asking for it?
3 What does 'quid' mean?
4 He suggests four different prices. Write them down.
5 She makes four offers. Write them down.

Some English sayings about money:

" Neither a borrower nor a lender be. "

From 'Hamlet' by William Shakespeare.

Have you ever borrowed money from anyone?
Who from? How much?

Have you ever lent money to anyone? Who to? How much?

Are you in debt at the moment? (i.e. Do you owe anyone any money?)

Does anyone owe you any money? Who? How much?

" Look after the pennies, and the pounds will look after themselves. "

Do you save money? Are you saving for anything at the moment? What?

Do you keep your money **a** in the bank? **b** in a safe? **c** in a money-box? **d** under the bed?

Have you got a bank account? Do you get any interest? What's the rate of interest? If you had a bank overdraft, how much interest would you have to pay?

" Live now – pay later. "

Have you bought anything on hire purchase? What? Did you pay a deposit? Do you think it's a good idea?

Have you got a credit card? Which one? (Visa? American Express? Diner's Club? Access?)

When you pay cash, do you ask for a discount? Do you usually get it?

" Annual income twenty pounds, annual expenditure nineteen nineteen and six, result happiness. Annual income twenty pounds, annual expenditure twenty pounds ought and six, result misery. "

Mr Micawber from 'David Copperfield' by Charles Dickens.

Do you spend more than you earn, or less than you earn?

Do you have a budget for your money?

Do you keep a record of your expenses?

" A fool and his money are soon parted. "

Where do you keep your money?
a in a purse **b** in a wallet **c** in a handbag **d** in a pocket

If you keep it in a pocket, which pocket do you keep it in?
a inside jacket-pocket
b back trouser-pocket
c side trouser-pocket
d top front jacket-pocket

Have you ever had your pocket picked?

When you stay in a hotel, do you hide your money? Where?
a in your suitcase **b** under the mattress **c** in the pillow **d** in a book **e** somewhere else

Is gambling legal or illegal in your country? Do people bet? What do they bet on?
a cards **b** horses **c** dogs **d** football **e** boxing **f** national lottery **e** something else

" The customer is always right. "

Have you bought anything this week? What?

What did it cost? Was it worth it?

Was it new or second-hand?

Was it a bargain? Did you get a receipt?

INSIDE STORY

"NEWS" REPORTER MISSING IN MANDANGA

Julian Snow, the 'Daily News' war correspondent, who is covering the civil war in Mandanga, has been reported missing.

He was last seen yesterday morning driving his Land Rover near the front line. The vehicle was found yesterday evening, but there was no sign of him. It is possible that he was ambushed and captured by guerilla forces. Snow has been a war correspondent for many years and has covered a number of conflicts, including Vietnam, Kampuchea, Zimbabwe and the Middle East.

STOP PRESS

JULIAN SNOW FREE War correspondent alive and well. Julian Snow walked into a government forces camp this morning, after spending two weeks with MLF (Mandanga Liberation Front) guerrillas. His exclusive story will appear in tomorrow's 'Daily News'.

IBC NEWS

This is IBC News. Julian Snow, the missing 'Daily News' reporter, was interviewed this morning by Dominic Beale of IBC News in Mandanga.

Beale Julian, can you tell us how you were captured in the first place?

Snow Well, I was on my way to visit a village near the front line. I came round a bend in the road and there was a tree lying across the road. I only just managed to stop in time! Suddenly, armed men appeared on all sides!

Beale What did you do?

Snow What would you do? I just sat there with my hands in the air! Anyway, they made me get out of the Land Rover, and made me lie on the ground ... I thought 'This is it! They're going to shoot me!' I started saying my prayers!

Beale What happened next?

Snow Well, they searched me. Of course, I didn't have any weapons, just a camera. It's funny, they let me keep it. Then they tied my hands together and blindfolded me. Then they made me get in the back of a truck and lie under some sacks. I've no idea where they took me, except that it was quite a large training camp. I was there for ten days.

Beale Were you treated well?

Snow Yes, I suppose I was. They let me walk about the camp and they let me take photographs, but they wouldn't let me photograph any faces. I was able to interview some of the leaders.

Beale How did you escape?

Snow I didn't! They put me back in the truck, blindfolded me again, drove for a few hours, then made me get out, pointed me in the direction of town and let me go!

Beale And what exactly did the guerrilla leaders say about the situation?

Snow Ah! Well, if you want to know that, you'll have to buy tomorrow's 'Daily News' ...

Exclusive!

JULIAN SNOW's inside story! In today's issue, Julian Snow tells his exclusive story. He was captured by Mandangan guerrillas two weeks ago. They forced him to go with them to their camp. However they allowed him to keep his camera, and to interview guerrilla leaders. Turn to page two for the story of his captivity!

Exercise

When I was younger, my parents made me go to bed early.
When I was younger, my parents didn't let me go out in the evenings.
Write true sentences about when you were younger.

PREFERENCES

A What are you doing tomorrow night?
B Nothing. Why?
A Well, do you like jazz?
B Yes, I do, very much.
A Which do you like best? Modern or traditional?
B I like both, really.
A There's a 'Weather Report' concert at the Hammersmith Odeon. Would you like to come?
B Oh, yes! They're my favourite group.

C Lisa, look over here. They've got a very good selection of Levi cords.
D Oh, yes! And they've got my size, too.
C But only in navy blue and black. Which do you prefer?
D Hmm. I don't like either of them very much. I really wanted green.
C They haven't got green in your size. Go on, try a pair on.
D No, no. I'd prefer to look somewhere else.

E Have you decided yet? What do you want to see?
F 'A Moment of Peace' is on at the Continental. I'd like to see that.
E Would you really? Oh, I'd rather see 'War in Space'.
F Oh, no! The reviews were terrible.
E I know, but it sounds fun. 'A Moment of Peace' is in French, and I'd rather not have to read subtitles.
F Then how about 'California Sunset'?
E I'd rather not ... I can't stand Steve Newman.
F Well, you choose.
E I don't fancy any of them. I'd much rather stay in and watch TV!

G What do you fancy?
H I don't know. There isn't much choice, is there?
G No, there isn't, really. What would you rather have? Steak and kidney or plaice?
H I can't make up my mind. I'd rather have a hamburger.
G We can ask for the full menu, if you like.
H No, it's not worth it. I'll have the plaice.

What's on in London

Jazz

Modern Jazz
★ **Weather Report** Hammersmith Odeon £2.50–£4 .

Traditional Jazz
★ **New Orleans Jazz Band**
'The Bull' Barnes 75p

Pop

Rock
★ **Ian Dury and the Blockheads**
Rainbow Theatre £3–£6

Reggae
★ **Burning Spear** Strand Lyceum £2.50–£4.50

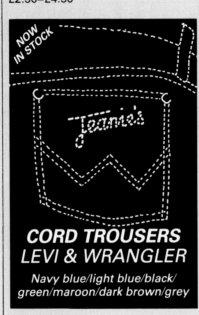

Cinema

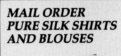

Ⓐ Ⓑ Ⓒ ❶ & ❷

❶ WAR IN SPACE (A)
2.00/5.15/8.15
❷ CIRCUS OF HORROR (X)
1.00/4.30/8.00

★ **Gaumont**
'California Sunset' (X)
Starring Steve Newman
3.10, 5.50, 8.30

★ **Continental**
'A Moment of Peace' (U)
(Jean le Brun) 1.10, 3.30, 6.00, 8.35

★ **Classic**
Humphrey Bogart in 'Casablanca' (A)
2.15, 4.15, 6.15, 8.15

★ **Odeon**
'Juke Box – 1958' (AA)
Separate programmes
2.45, 5.30, 8.20

37

Unit 17

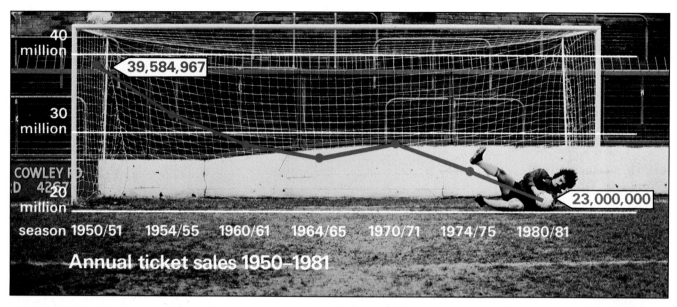

Annual ticket sales 1950–1981

40 million
30 million
20 million

39,584,967

23,000,000

season 1950/51 1954/55 1960/61 1964/65 1970/71 1974/75 1980/81

WHERE HAVE ALL THE FANS GONE?

'Good evening and welcome to the 'Michael Parkhurst Talkabout'. In tonight's 'Talkabout' we're looking at the problem of soccer's missing millions. Since 1950 attendance at football matches has fallen by nearly fifty per cent. Many clubs are in financial trouble, and tonight we hope to identify the major causes and discuss some possible solutions.

First of all, we'll hear from one of soccer's lost millions, Mr Bert Woods from London, who used to be a regular Chelsea supporter.'

'I stopped going five or six years ago. I'd rather stay at home and watch it on telly. You get a better view and I like the action replays. I'm too afraid to go now, really! All this violence, you know. When I was a lad there was the occasional fight on the terraces, but nothing like you see these days – whole gangs of teenagers who aren't interested in football. Somebody ought to do something about it! These kids aren't real fans, they just come looking for trouble. The police ought to sort out the real fans from the troublemakers. You know, I always used to go with my dad, but I wouldn't take my kids. There's too much foul language. And I don't only blame the kids. There ought to be more discipline at home and in schools.'

'Thank you, Mr Woods. Let's go over to Brian Huff, the manager of Eastfield United, one of our most successful clubs. Brian.'

'I sympathize with Mr Woods, and there are plenty of people like him. Anyway, we'd better do something about it, or we'll all go broke! The clubs and players must share the blame. Football's big business, and it's very competitive. Winning has become the most important thing. There's too much violence on the field. Referees have to get tougher with players. They should send off players for deliberate fouls. The other problem is television. There's too much football on TV, and they only show the most exciting parts, goals, fouls and violence. People are bored when they see the real game. Anyway the clubs started talking about these problems ten years ago, and nothing's been done. We'd better not spend another ten years talking. We'd better do something, and do it soon!'

'Our next guest is a young fan. Kevin Dolan, a Manchester United supporter, who is sixteen years old. What do you think, Kevin?'

'Well I'm not one of soccer's missing millions. I never miss a match. I've travelled all over the country with United and I've never been in trouble. I blame the media for most of this violence. They only show young people when they're doing something wrong. They ought not to give so much publicity to trouble-makers. It only encourages the others, doesn't it? The violence always starts when there's a TV camera near. If they banned alcohol from football grounds, there'd be much less trouble.'

'Thank you, Kevin. Our last speaker is Jimmy MacTavish, the ex-Scotland striker who has just returned from the United States after spending two years with Miami Galaxy. Well, Jimmy. What ought we to do?'

'I agree with a lot of what's been said, Michael, but hadn't we better look at some solutions? I've been playing in the States for the last two seasons and I haven't seen any violence over there. A football match is a day out for the family. More than half the supporters are women and children, and there are much better facilities. Everybody gets a comfortable seat. There are good restaurants and there's entertainment before and after the game, and at half-time. Football stadiums are old, cold and dirty over here. We'd better take a good look at American soccer. I think we've got a lot to learn! Entertainment is what football is all about and we'd better not forget it!'

Exercise
Find words which mean:
1 television or TV
2 forbidden
3 not accidental
4 stadium
5 boy
6 young person or child
7 disgusting
8 without money
9 an action against the rules
10 share the same feelings

NIGHT FLIGHT

'This is Captain Cook speaking. Our estimated time of arrival in Brisbane will be one a.m., so we've got a long flight ahead of us. I hope you enjoy it. Our hostesses will be serving dinner shortly. Thank you.'

It was Christmas Eve 1959, and the beginning of another routine flight. The hostesses started preparing the food trays. A few of the passengers were trying to get some sleep, but most of them were reading. There was nothing to see from the windows except the vast blackness of the Australian desert below. There was nothing unusual about the flight, except perhaps that the plane was nearly full. A lot of the passengers were travelling home to spend Christmas with their families. The hostesses started serving dinner.

It was a smooth and quiet flight. The hostesses had finished collecting the trays, and they were in the galley putting things away when the first buzzers sounded. One of the hostesses went along the aisle to check. When she came back she looked surprised. 'It's amazing,' she said. 'Even on a smooth flight like this two people have been sick.'

Twenty minutes later nearly half the passengers were ill – dramatically ill. Several were moaning and groaning, some were doubled up in pain, and two were unconscious. Fortunately there was a doctor on board, and he was helping the hostesses. He came to the galley and said, 'I'd better speak to the captain. This is a severe case of food poisoning. I think we'd better land as soon as possible.' 'What caused it?' asked one of the hostesses. 'Well,' replied the doctor, 'I had the beef for dinner, and I'm fine. The passengers who chose the fish are ill.' The hostess led him to the flight deck. She tried to open the door. 'I think it's jammed,' she said. The doctor helped her to push it open. The captain was

lying behind the door. He was unconscious. The co-pilot was slumped across the controls, and the radio operator was trying to revive him.

The doctor quickly examined the two pilots. 'They just collapsed,' said the radio operator. 'I don't feel too good myself.' 'Can you land the plane?' said the doctor. 'Me? No, I'm not a pilot. We've got to revive them!' he replied. 'The plane's on automatic pilot. We're OK for a couple of hours.' 'I don't know,' said the doctor. 'They could be out for a long time.' 'I'd better contact ground control,' said the radio operator. The doctor turned to the hostess. 'Perhaps you should make an announcement, try to find out if there's a pilot on board.' 'We can't do that!' she said, 'It'll cause a general panic.' 'Well how the hell are we going to get this thing down?' said the doctor.

Suddenly the hostess remembered something. 'One of the passengers . . . I overheard him saying that he'd been a pilot in the war. I'll get him.' She found the man and asked him to come to the galley. 'Didn't you say you used to be a pilot?' she asked. 'Yes . . . why? The pilot's all right, isn't he?' She led him to the flight deck. They explained the situation to him. 'You mean, you want me to fly the plane?' he said. 'You must be joking. I was a pilot, but I flew single-engined fighter planes, and that was fifteen years ago. This thing's got four engines!'

'Isn't there anybody else?' he asked. 'I'm afraid not,' said the hostess. The man sat down at the controls. His hands were shaking slightly. The radio operator connected him to Air Traffic Control. They told him to keep flying on automatic pilot towards Brisbane, and to wait for further instructions from an experienced pilot. An hour later the lights of Brisbane appeared on the horizon. He could see the lights of the runway shining brightly beyond the city. Air Traffic Control told him to keep circling until the fuel gauge registered almost empty. This gave him a chance to get used to handling the controls. In the cabin the hostesses and the doctor were busy attending to the sick. Several people were unconscious. The plane circled for over half an hour. The passengers had begun to realize that something was wrong. 'What's going on? Why don't we

land?' shouted a middle-aged man. 'My wife's ill. We've got to get her to hospital!' A woman began sobbing quietly. At last the plane started its descent. Suddenly there was a bump which shook the plane. 'We're all going to die!' screamed a man. Even the hostesses looked worried as panic began to spread through the plane. 'It's all right!' someone said, 'The pilot's just lowered the wheels, that's all.' As the plane approached the runway they could see fire trucks and ambulances speeding along beside the runway with their lights flashing. There was a tremendous thump as the wheels hit the tarmac, bounced twice, raced along the runway and screeched to a halt. The first airport truck was there in seconds. 'That was nearly a perfect landing. Well done!' shouted the control tower. 'Thanks,' said the man. 'Any chance of a job?'

THE JUNK-SHOP

Justin Wedgewood and Lenny Smith are antique-dealers. They've got a very successful business. They travel around the country buying antique furniture and paintings from junk-shops and from elderly people, and then they sell them from their shop in Kensington, a fashionable part of London. Today they're in a small Welsh town. Justin's just come out of a little junk-shop, and he seems very excited.

Justin Lenny, we're in luck! There's a painting in there, a landscape, it's a good one. I thought it might be valuable, so I had a good look at the signature. It isn't very clear. I think it may be a Constable.

Lenny A Constable? It can't be! They're all in art galleries. They're worth a fortune!

Justin Well, someone found one two years ago. This might be another. It's dirty and it isn't in very good condition.

Lenny How much do you think it's worth?

Justin I don't know. It may be worth a hundred thousand, it might even be worth more!

Lenny Be careful, Justin. We'd better use the old trick.

Justin Right. There's a chair in the window. It must be worth about five pounds. I'll offer the old lady fifty quid for it. She'll be so pleased that she won't think about the painting.

Lenny Don't say you want the painting, say you want the frame. OK?

Justin Fine, you'd better wait in the van. I'd rather do this on my own.

Lenny Er ... Justin, check the signature before you give her fifty quid for the chair.

Justin Don't worry, Lenny. I know what I'm doing.

Mrs Griffiths I'll be with you in a minute.

Justin Hello. I'm interested in that chair in the window.

Mrs Griffiths What? That old thing? It's been there for years!

Justin Has it? Er ... it's very nice. I think it could be Victorian.

Mrs Griffiths Really?

Justin Yes, I think I'm right. I've seen one or two other chairs like it. I think I could get a good price for that in London. I'll offer you fifty pounds.

Mrs Griffiths Fifty! You must be mad, man!

Justin No, no. It's a fair price.

Mrs Griffiths Well, then, it's yours.

Justin There you are then, fifty pounds. Goodbye. Oh, by the way, that painting's in a nice frame.

Mrs Griffiths It's a nice picture, dear. Early nineteenth century, I've heard.

Justin Oh, no ... no, it can't be. I've seen lots like it. It must be twentieth century. There's no market for them. Still, I could use the frame.

Mrs Griffiths All right. How much will you give me for it?

Justin Er ... how about twenty pounds?

Mrs Griffiths Oh, no, dear. It must be worth more than that. It came from the big house on the hill.

Justin Did it? Let me have another look at it. Yes, the frame is really nice. I'll give you a hundred.

Mrs Griffiths Oh, dear, I don't know what to do. You see, I like that painting myself.

Justin All right, a hundred and twenty. That's my final offer.

Mrs Griffiths Shall we say ... a hundred and fifty?

Justin OK. It's a deal.

Mrs Griffiths Shall I wrap it for you?

Justin No, no. I've got the van outside. It was nice doing business with you. Goodbye!

Mrs Griffiths Bye-bye, dear. Thank you.

Mrs Griffiths Owen?

Mr Griffiths Yes, my love?

Mrs Griffiths I've sold another of your imitation Constables. You'd better bring another one downstairs, if the paint's dry. The gentleman who bought it seemed very pleased with it.

Look at this

I'm certain ...	It must be ...
I'm almost certain ...	

I think it's possible ...	It could be ...
	It may be ...

I think it's possible ... (but a little less possible than 'may')	It might be ...

I think it's nearly impossible ...	It can't be ...
I think it's impossible ...	

NOISY NEIGHBOURS

Sybil Sidney! Sidney! Wake up!

Sidney Eh! What? What's the matter? It can't be eight o'clock already!

Sybil No, it's half past one. It's those people next door again. Listen!

Sidney Oh, yes. They must be having another party.

Sybil Listen to that! They must be waking up the whole street. And they've got three young children. They can't be sleeping through that noise. It's disgusting! Somebody should call the police! Sidney, wake up!

Sidney Eh? I wasn't asleep, dear. They're all laughing. They must be having a good time! They never invite us, do they?

Sybil Sidney!

Sidney Yes, dear. What is it now?

Sybil Listen! They must be leaving.

Sidney Thank goodness for that! Maybe we'll get some sleep.

Sybil I hope so. It's nearly three o'clock. Goodnight, dear.

Sidney Oh, hell! They're having a row, now.

Sybil I'm not surprised. They always have rows after parties.

Sybil Oh! They must be throwing the pots and pans again.

Sidney No, I think that was a plate, dear, or maybe the television. They'll be sorry in the morning.

Sybil Sidney! Wake up!

Sidney Eh! Oh, what's that?

Sybil He can't be hammering at this time of night.

Sybil What time is it?

Sybil Four o'clock. What can they be doing at four o'clock in the morning?

Sidney I can't hear any voices. Go back to sleep, Sybil.

Sybil Sidney! Listen. There's someone in the garden next door.

Sidney Eh? It must be the milkman.

Sybil No, it can't be. It's too early. It's only quarter to five. Who could it be? You'd better have a look.

Sidney All right. Ooh! It's Mr Sykes, and he's carrying a spade.

Sybil Oh, no! You don't think he's killed her, do you?

Sidney Well, we haven't heard her voice for a while. No, she's probably sleeping.

Sybil But what can he be doing at this time of night?

Sydney If he has killed her, he might be burying the body!

Sybil What! You don't think so, do you?

Sidney Well, he can't be planting potatoes, can he? I suppose you want me to phone the police?

Sybil No. Ask him what he's doing first!

Sidney Hello, there, Mr Sykes. You're up early this morning.

Mr Sykes I haven't been to bed yet. We had a party last night. I hope we didn't keep you awake.

Sidney Oh, no. We didn't hear anything, nothing at all.

Mr Sykes Well, it was a pretty noisy party. My wife knocked over the goldfish tank while we were clearing up. The poor fish died. I'm just burying them before the children wake up.

Exercise

What do you think your parents/brothers/sisters/friends are doing at this moment?

If you think you know what they are doing answer with:

They must be doing this.
They can't be doing that.
They're probably doing this.

If you don't know, use:
They could/may/might be doing this.
or:
They're possibly doing this.

What about the President of the USA/the Queen of England/the students in the class next door/the director of the school/a famous pop star/a famous sports personality?

YOU'RE IN THE ARMY NOW!

It's Saturday afternoon at Botherington Army Camp. The new recruits are supposed to be working, but they aren't. The Colonel's away today and they're lazing around in the barracks. The Sergeant-Major has just opened the door. He's brought the duty roster with him, so he knows exactly what each of them should be doing.

Sergeant-Major 'Hello, hello ... what's going on here?'

Exercise 1

Look at Smith in the picture. Ask and answer about the other soldiers.

1 *What's he doing?*
  He's sitting on the bed.
  He's drinking.
  He's listening to the radio.
2 *Should he be drinking?*
  No he shouldn't.
  Should he be mowing the grass?
  Yes, he should.
3 *What should he be doing?*
  He should be mowing the grass.
  What shouldn't he be doing?
  He shouldn't be sitting on the bed.
  He shouldn't be drinking.
  He shouldn't be listening to the radio.

Exercise 2

Smith ought to be mowing the grass, he ought not to be drinking.
Write similar sentences about the other soldiers.

Sergeant-Major Smith! What are you doing?
Smith I'm listening to the radio, sir.
Sergeant-Major And what are you supposed to be doing, Smith?
Smith I'm not sure, sir.
Sergeant-Major Well, let me tell you, Smith. You are supposed to be mowing the lawn!
Smith Yes, sir. I'm sorry sir. It won't happen again, sir.
Sergeant-Major It'd better not, Smith. And when I come back, Smith, you'd better be mowing that grass! Do you understand?
Smith Yes, sir.
Sergeant-Major This isn't a holiday camp. You're in the army now!

Exercise 3

Make similar conversations between the Sergeant-Major and the other soldiers.

Look at this.

SMITH

JONES

MURPHY

McCOY

KILROY

Exercise 4

Smith's mowing the grass.
He'd rather not be mowing the grass.
He'd rather be lying on the beach.
Make sentences about the other soldiers.

Exercise 5

What are you doing?
What would you rather be doing?
Make five sentences.

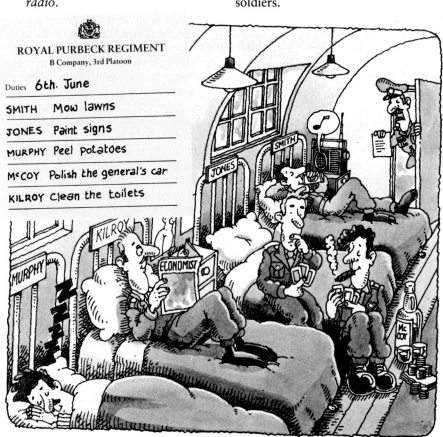

ROYAL PURBECK REGIMENT
B Company, 3rd Platoon

Duties **6th. June**

SMITH   Mow lawns
JONES   Paint signs
MURPHY   Peel potatoes
McCOY   Polish the general's car
KILROY   Clean the toilets

MIGRATION

One of the greatest mysteries of nature is the instinct to migrate. Every year millions of creatures feel the need to move for one reason or another. Most of us have seen the arrival or departure of migrating flocks of birds. Migration, however, is not confined to birds, but can be seen in reptiles (for example turtles, frogs), insects (butterflies, locusts), fish (eels, salmon, tunny) and mammals (reindeer, seals, lemmings, whales, bats). Many of these creatures succeed in navigating over long distances. How exactly they manage to do this still remains a mystery. There are several possibilities. They may navigate by using one or more of the following:

1 The sun.
2 The stars.
3 The Earth's magnetic field. (When a small bar magnet is attached to a pigeon, it is unable to navigate.)
4 A sense of smell.
5 Geographical features. (Birds flying from North Africa to France seem to follow coastlines and valleys.)
6 Changes in temperature. (Salmon can detect a change in water temperature as small as 0.03°C.)
7 Sound. (Whales and bats seem to use sonar.)

Experiments suggest that these navigational abilities are partly instinctive. In one famous experiment a young seabird from the island of Skokholm, off the Welsh coast, was taken across the Atlantic by plane to Boston, 5100 km away. It was released, and was back in its nest twelve and a half days later.

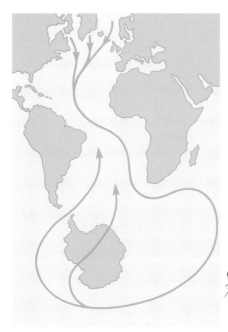

The Arctic Tern

This seabird holds the record for long-distance migration. Arctic Tern breed in Northern Canada, Greenland, Northern Europe, Siberia and Alaska. In late August they set off on a 17,500 km journey which takes them south, past the West coasts of Europe and Africa to the tip of Southern Africa (14,000 km in 90 days). They then fly round to the Indian Ocean and down to Antarctica, where they spend the Antarctic summer. On the way back they sometimes make a complete circuit of Antarctica before returning to their breeding-grounds. The round trip is over 35,000 km in eight months (240 km a day when they are flying.) The Arctic Tern sees more hours of daylight than any other creature, because it experiences two summers a year, one in the Arctic region, and one in the Antarctic. These regions have almost constant daylight in summer. One tern, which was ringed in Norway as a chick, died in exactly the same place, twenty-seven years later. Presumably, it had made the journey twenty-seven times.

The European Freshwater Eel

European Freshwater Eels, which look like snakes but are really fish, begin and end their lives in the Sargasso Sea, southeast of Bermuda. As eggs and larvae they drift for three years towards Europe, changing both shape and colour as they reach the fresh-water estuaries of European rivers. They spend the next nine to nineteen years in rivers, streams, lakes and ponds. As they approach old age they seem to have an unexplained compulsion to return to the Sargasso Sea to breed. Many eels which have found their way into ponds and lakes come out of the water and travel overland, gliding through damp grass. When they reach the sea, they make their way to the Sargasso, where they breed and die. No eels make the journey twice. The eel has an acute sense of smell, which is used for navigation in local waters, but inherited memory seems the only explanation for their migration to the Sargasso.

The Lemming

The Brown Lemming is a small mammal (10–18cm long) found all over Northern Canada, Scandinavia and Northern Russia. Lemmings usually make short, annual migrations in spring, travelling by night and feeding and sleeping by day. Every three or four years, however, they make much longer migrations in large numbers. The lemming population seems to change over a three or four year cycle, from one lemming per four hectares to between 400 and 700 lemmings per four hectares. Migration seems to be a method of population control, and is most spectacular in the well-known 'mass suicides', where thousands of lemmings plunge over cliff tops into the sea, and swim till they die of exhaustion. These 'mass suicides' only occur infrequently, and then only in Norway where mountains touch the sea. Nobody knows what makes them do it, but there are two theories. One is that migrating lemmings cross rivers and lakes and can't tell the difference between a river and the sea. The other, more interesting theory is that they are migrating towards ancient breeding-grounds which existed beneath the North Sea millions of years ago, when the sea-level was lower.

MURDER AT GURNEY

Part 1

Lord Gurney was found dead on the library floor of his country house in Norfolk. He had been shot five times. The police have been called. There are six people in the house and they all heard the shots at about nine o'clock. The police have taken statements and made the following notes about each of the six people.

Lady Agatha Gurney, 62

Married to Lord Gurney for thirty-five years.
Disabled – has been in a wheel-chair since a riding accident, twelve years ago.
Very jealous woman.
Had a row with Celia Smart in the afternoon.
Told Lord Gurney to sack her.
After long argument, Lord Gurney refused to sack her.

Lady Agatha's statement.
I was in my room. My bedroom's on the ground floor because I can't walk. I was reading. I heard the shots; there were four or five. I wheeled myself into the hall. The door of the library was open. Miss Smart was standing in the doorway, screaming. Gillespie was standing at the French windows. The gun was on the floor by the body.

Celia Smart, 24

Secretary to Lord Gurney.
Young, beautiful, intelligent – works to support her sick mother.
Employed by Lord Gurney for a year.
Report in gossip column in today's 'Daily News' that she had been seen last Saturday with Tristan Gurney at a new disco, 'The Charteris Club' in London's Mayfair.
Lord Gurney very angry about it.
Threatened to sack her, but didn't.

Celia Smart's statement.
I was in the drawing-room, writing some letters, job applications actually. I heard the shots, ran across the hall, the library door was open ... poor dear Horace was lying in a pool of blood. I started screaming. Gillespie came in through the French windows, they were open. Then Lady Agatha arrived. She didn't say a word. She just stared at me.

Tristan Gurney, 33

Lord Gurney's only son.
Reputation as a playboy and international gambler.
Thrown out of boarding-school and the army.
Has large gambling debts.
Arrested last year for possessing drugs.
Is heir to the Gurney estate – will inherit £2 million.
Lord Gurney had refused to give him any more money.

Tristan's statement.
I was in the billiard room. I was practising. Suddenly there were five shots. I thought it was Chivers shooting birds in the garden again, Then I heard a scream. It sounded like Celia, so I opened the connecting door to the library and saw father lying there, Gillespie at the window, and Celia and mother together in the main doorway. I couldn't believe my eyes.

Major Chivers, 60

At school and in the army with Lord Gurney.
Was army pistol-shooting champion.
Drinks heavily.
Drives a Bentley.
Doesn't work – spends time shooting and fishing.
Was Managing-Director of Gurney Property Ltd.
Went to prison for two years when the company collapsed with debts of £½ million after a big property scandal.
Has lived at Gurney Manor since leaving prison.

Major Chivers' statement.
I was by the lake, fishing in my usual place. When I heard the shots, I hurried through the trees towards the house. I saw Gillespie running across the lawn towards the library. When I got there, everybody was in the room, except Tom Giles, the gardener. Poor old Gurney was dead. I was absolutely sure he was dead. After all, I was in the army for twenty years.

Gillespie, 65

Butler. Has worked for the Gurneys for nearly fifty years.
Retires in two months.
Likes good wine and good food.
Takes Lady Agatha out every day in her wheelchair.
Knows everything about the family.
Had long argument with Lord Gurney in the morning.
Knows Celia Smart's father very well – introduced her to Lord Gurney.

Gillespie's statement.
I was taking my evening walk. I had just come out of the kitchen door, I was walking round the corner of the house when I heard shooting. I ran across the lawn to the French windows. I saw Lord Gurney's body, and Miss Smart in the doorway.

Tom Giles, 29

Gardener.
Often goes fishing with the Major.
Proposed marriage to Celia Smart, but was rejected.
Been in trouble with the police several times, for fighting in the village pub.
Has a violent temper.
Had argument about a pay rise earlier in the day.

Tom Giles' statement.
I was working in the kitchen garden. I heard shots, but that's not unusual around here. Lord Gurney and the Major are very fond of shooting. Then I heard lots of screaming and shouting, so I went into the house through the kitchen door to see what was happening. They were all there. I wasn't sorry. He deserved it. Everybody hated him.

MANOR

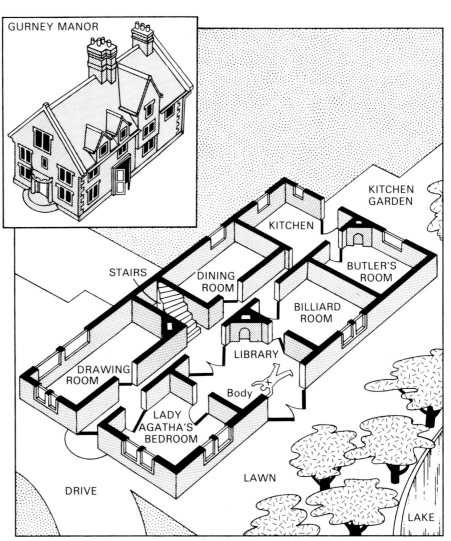

GURNEY MANOR

KITCHEN GARDEN

KITCHEN

BUTLER'S ROOM

STAIRS

DINING ROOM

BILLIARD ROOM

LIBRARY

DRAWING ROOM

Body +

LADY AGATHA'S BEDROOM

LAWN

DRIVE

LAKE

Part 2

Inspector Marples is in charge of the case. Sergeant Watts is his assistant. They're in the library.

Marples Where is everybody, Sergeant?

Watts They're all in the drawing-room, sir. Constable Dickson's with them. What do you think, sir?

Marples It could have been any one of them, couldn't it? We don't know what skeletons are in the cupboard! It may have been two of them together. It might even have been all of them. Nobody seems very sad!

Watts No, sir. Lord Gurney was a very unpopular man in the village. Nobody liked him. It could have been an outsider.

Marples No, no, Watts. It must have been one of them. Let's look at the evidence.

Watts It seems to me that everybody has got a motive, sir, and nobody's got an alibi. They all say they were alone when it happened.

Marples Yes, and there are no fingerprints on the gun.

Lady Agatha?

Watts It couldn't have been her, sir.

Marples Why not, Watts?

Watts Well, she's in a wheelchair. She can't move very fast. Anyway, they've been married for thirty-five years. It can't have been her.

Marples Most murders are inside the family, Watts, and there is a door between her room and the library.

Watts Ah, yes, sir. But it was locked!

Marples Doors have keys, Watts!

Watts But why would she want to kill him?

Marples Miss Smart's a very attractive young woman. We don't know what was going on. She could have been jealous.

Watts But, sir, he was over sixty! He was old enough to be her father!

Marples Ah, well, Watts, he was a good-looking man, and very rich!

Major Chivers?

Marples What about the Major, Watts? He's a strange fellow.

Watts I've been thinking about that. It can't have been him, sir!

Marples Really! Why not?

Watts Why would he need to fire five times? He was an army pistol champion. He could have killed him with one shot.

Marples Maybe he did, Watts. Maybe he did.

Watts I don't understand, sir.

Marples There are a lot of things you don't understand, Watts. Perhaps he's more clever than he looks.

Watts But there's no motive, sir.

Marples There may have been. I mean there was that scandal with the property company.

Watts But he was at the lake, sir.

Marples He might not have been, Watts. He's a pistol champion. He could have shot him from the trees and thrown the gun into the room.

Watts Oh. Do you really think so, sir?

Marples I don't know, Watts. It's just a theory.

Look at this

Can Could	it have been	him? her? them?

It	must could may (not) might (not) can't couldn't	have been	him. her. them.

Can Could	he she they	have	done it? killed him? shot him?

He She They	must could may (not) might (not) can't couldn't	have	done it. killed him. shot him.

Exercise

Discuss each character. Make a list of sentences about all six suspects. Who do you think did it? How? Why?

KNOW YOUR RIGHTS

Complaining about faulty goods or bad service is never easy. Most people dislike making a fuss. However, when you are shopping, it is important to know your rights. The following extract is taken from a leaflet produced by the British 'Office of Fair Trading', and it gives advice to consumers.

Your rights when buying goods

When you buy something from a shop, you are making a contract. This contract means that it's up to the shop – not the manufacturer – to deal with your complaints if the goods are not satisfactory. What do we mean by satisfactory?

The goods must not be broken or damaged and must work properly. This is known as 'merchantable quality'. A sheet, say, which had a tear in it, or a clock that didn't go when you wound it would not pass this test.

The goods must be as described – whether on the pack or by the salesman. A hairdryer which the box says is blue should not turn out to be pink; a pair of shoes the salesman says is leather should not be plastic.

The goods should be fit for their purpose. This means the purpose for which most people buy those particular goods. If you wanted something for a special purpose, you must have said exactly what for. If, for instance, the shop assures you that a certain glue will mend broken china, and it doesn't you have a right to return it.

If the shop sells you faulty goods, it has broken its side of the bargain.

If things go wrong

If goods are faulty when you first inspect or use them, go back to the shop, say that you cancel the purchase and ask for a complete refund. If you prefer, you can accept a repair or a replacement.

If the goods break down through no fault of yours, after you have used them for a time, you may still be entitled to some compensation. In some cases it would be reasonable to expect a complete refund – if, for instance, without misuse your shoes came apart after only one day's wear, or your washing machine irreparably broke down after only three wash days. But if your washing machine worked perfectly for a while and then broke, you could only expect some of the purchase price back. You and the supplier must negotiate a reasonable settlement.

You need never accept a credit note for faulty goods. If you do so, then later find you do not want anything else in the shop or store, you may not get your money back.

If you have to spend money as a direct result of goods being faulty, you can also claim this from the shop. You could, for example, claim the cost of using a laundry while the washing machine wasn't working. But you must keep such expenses down to a minimum.

There are four golden rules:

1 Examine the goods you buy at once. If they are faulty, tell the seller quickly.

2 Keep any receipts you are given. If you have to return something, the receipt will help to prove where and when you bought it.

3 Don't be afraid to complain. You are not asking a favour to have faulty goods put right. The law is on your side.

4 Be persistent (but not aggressive). If your complaint is justified, it is somebody's responsibility to put things right.

Remember

● You can't complain about defects that were pointed out to you, or that you could reasonably have been expected to notice.

● Stop using the item as soon as you discover a fault.

● You are not entitled to compensation if you simply change your mind about wanting the goods.

MAKING A COMPLAINT

Customer Good morning, miss. I'd like to speak to the manager.

Manager I am the manager, sir. How can I help you?

Customer Oh, really? It's this radio. It doesn't work.

Manager Mm ... did you buy it here?

Customer Pardon? Of course I bought it here. Look, you switch it on and nothing happens.

Manager Could I see your receipt?

Customer Receipt? I haven't got one.

Manager Oh, you should have obtained a receipt when you bought it.

Customer I probably did. I must have thrown it away.

Manager Ah, well, have you got any other proof of purchase, the guarantee, for example?

Customer No. It must have been in the box. I threw that away too.

Manager Oh, dear. You really ought to have kept it. We need to know the exact date of purchase.

Customer What? I only bought it yesterday! That young man over there served me. Oh, I paid by cheque. I've got the cheque stub.

Manager That's all right then. Did you check the radio before you left the shop?

Customer Check it? No, it was in the box. I expected it to work. It wasn't a cheap radio, it's a good make.

Manager You should have checked it.

Customer Come on! Stop telling me what I should have done, and do something! Either give me my money back or give me another radio.

Manager There's no need to get aggressive, sir. Let me look at it ... mm ... you see this little switch on the back?

Customer Yes?

Manager It's on 'mains', and it should be on 'battery'. You really should have read the instructions.

Customer Oh!

97 Cuckoo Lane,
Tunbridge Wells,
Kent

22nd May, 1982

Customer Service Dept.,
Dicken's Electrical Ltd.,
Harlow,
Essex

Dear Sir or Madam,

Last week I bought a pocket calculator at your branch in Cheltenham. It seemed to work in the shop. When I got home, I found that it was faulty. It adds and subtracts perfectly well, but it does not divide or multiply. I took it back to your branch in Tunbridge Wells, but they refused to exchange it, saying that I would have to return it to the branch where I bought it. This is impossible because I do not live in Cheltenham. Please find enclosed the calculator, together with the receipt, showing price and date of purchase, and the manufacturer's guarantee.

Yours faithfully,

C. R. S. Sketchley

Exercise

DIGITAL ALARM CLOCK

This product should reach you in perfect working order. If it does not, please return it to Electric Clocks Ltd., Hounslow, Middlesex, stating where and when it was bought. We will be glad to exchange it and refund the postage.

Write a letter of complaint. You bought the clock at a branch of W. H. Samson in Oxford Street, London, last week. It said 'blue' on the box, but it was pink. The alarm doesn't seem to work. You paid cash, and you didn't keep the receipt.

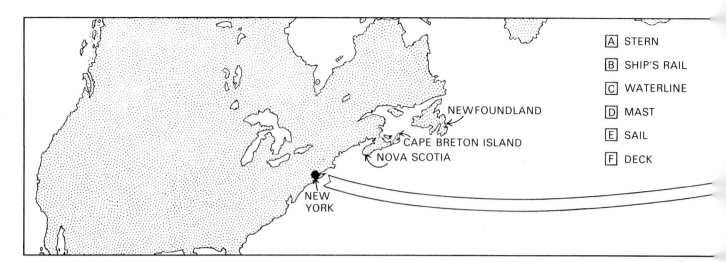

A	STERN
B	SHIP'S RAIL
C	WATERLINE
D	MAST
E	SAIL
F	DECK

THE 'MARY CELESTE'

The 'Mary Celeste' was built in 1861 in Nova Scotia, Canada, as a cargo-carrying sailing-ship. When it was launched, it was given the name 'The Amazon'. It was not a lucky ship. The first captain died a few days after it was registered, and on its first voyage in 1862 it was badly damaged in a collision. While it was being repaired in port, it caught fire. In 1863 it crossed the Atlantic for the first time, and in the English Channel it collided with another ship which sank. 'The Amazon' was badly damaged itself. Four years later, in 1867, it ran aground on Cape Breton Island, off the Canadian coast. The ship was almost completely wrecked and had to be rebuilt. It was then sold and the name was changed to the 'Mary Celeste'. Sailors are very superstitious and dislike sailing on ships which have been unlucky or which have changed their names. Many sailors refused to sail on the 'Mary Celeste'.

On November 5th 1872, the 'Mary Celeste' left New York, carrying a cargo of commercial alcohol to Genoa in Italy. There were eleven people on board, Captain Briggs, his wife and two-year-old daughter, and a crew of eight. Briggs was an experienced captain, and a very religious man. In his cabin there was a harmonium, which was used for playing hymns. A month later the 'Mary Celeste' was seen by another ship, the 'Dei Gratia', about halfway between the Azores and the Portuguese coast.

Captain Moorhouse of the 'Dei Gratia', a friend of Captain Briggs, noticed that the ship was sailing strangely. When the 'Mary Celeste' did not answer his signal, he decided to investigate. He sent a small boat to find out what was wrong.

The 'Mary Celeste' was completely deserted.
☞ The only lifeboat was missing.
☞ All the sails were up, and in good condition.
☞ All the cargo was there.
☞ The ship had obviously been through storms. The glass on the compass was broken.
☞ The windows of the deck cabins had been covered with wooden planks.
☞ There was a metre of water in the cargo hold, which was not enough to be dangerous.
☞ The water pumps were working perfectly.
☞ There was enough food for six months, and plenty of fresh water.
☞ All the crew's personal possessions (clothes, boots, pipes and tobacco etc.) were on board.
☞ There were toys on the captain's bed.
☞ There was food and drink on the cabin table.
☞ Only the navigation instruments and ship's papers were missing.
☞ The last entry in the ship's log-book had been made eleven days earlier, 1000 km west, but the ship had continued in a straight line.

☞ The fore-hatch was found open.
☞ There were two deep marks on the bows, near the water-line.
☞ There was a deep cut on the ship's rail, made by an axe.
☞ There were old brown bloodstains on the deck, and on the captain's sword, which was in the cabin.

Captain Moorhouse put some sailors on the 'Mary Celeste', who sailed it to Portugal. There was a long official investigation, but the story of what had happened on the ship, and what had happened to the crew, still remains a mystery. Captain Moorhouse and his crew were given the salvage money for bringing the ship to port. Many explanations have been suggested, but none of them have ever been proved.

Exercise
Find words which mean:
1 All the people working on a ship.
2 The official, daily, written record of a ship's voyage.
3 A religious song.
4 Put a boat into the water.
5 An instrument that shows the position of 'north'.
6 A musical instrument, like a small organ.
7 A long, thin, narrow, flat piece of wood.
8 Payment given to those who save others' property at sea.
9 Goods carried on a ship.
10 A machine for forcing water into or out of something.

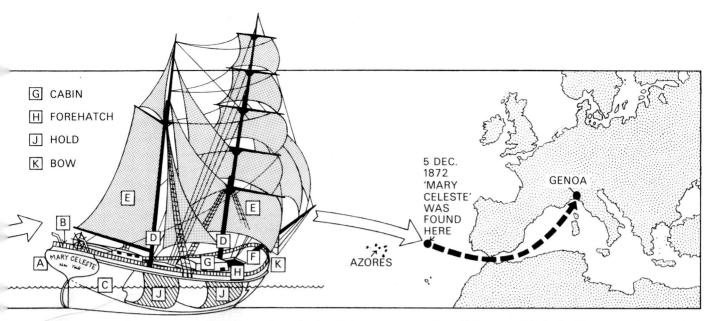

G CABIN
H FOREHATCH
J HOLD
K BOW

5 DEC. 1872 'MARY CELESTE' WAS FOUND HERE

GENOA

AZORES

What do you think happened?

Sarah I don't know what happened, but it must have happened suddenly.

Mark Why do you think that?

Sarah Think about it. There were toys on the captain's bed, weren't there? The child must have been playing, and they must have interrupted her suddenly.

Mark Yes, that's true. And the food was on the table. They must have been eating, or getting ready to eat.

Sarah I'll tell you my theory. The lifeboat was missing, right? They could have been practising their emergency drill. They must have got into the boat, and launched it.

Mark All right, but what happened to the boat?

Sarah Ah! They may have been rowing the lifeboat round the ship, and there must have been a gust of wind, then the ship could have moved forward and run down the lifeboat. That explains the marks on the bows!

Mark Come on! They can't all have been sitting in the lifeboat. What about the captain? He should have been steering the ship!

Sarah Ah, he might have been watching the drill, and jumped in to save the others!

Some possible explanations of why the crew abandoned the ship.

Amazingly, all of these have been suggested at some time.

1 There was water in the hold. The crew panicked and abandoned the ship because they thought it was going to sink. (Why? The captain was very experienced, and the ship was in good condition. The water-pumps were working.)

2 The child fell into the sea. The mother jumped in to save her. They launched a lifeboat to rescue her. (All of them? Why?)

3 One of the barrels of alcohol was damaged. Perhaps there was a small explosion. The hatch cover was off, either because of the explosion or to let the gas escape. They thought all the cargo might explode. (But not much evidence of an explosion.)

4 The last log entry was 1000 km west, near Santa Maria Island. Maybe the ship was in danger of running aground on the island. The crew left the ship in a storm. (How did the ship continue in a straight line for eleven days?)

5 There was no wind, so they got into the lifeboat to tow the ship. The rope broke. (Why were the woman and child in the lifeboat? Surely the ship was too heavy?)

6 They saw an island which was not on the map, and went to investigate. (All of them?)

7 One of the crew had a terrible, infectious disease. The others left to escape from it. The one with the disease killed himself.

What about the lifeboat?

If the crew left the ship by lifeboat, what happened to them?

1 It could have sunk in a storm.

2 The ship itself could have run down the lifeboat.

3 It could have drifted away, and all of them could have died of hunger and thirst.

4 They might have reached land. They were robbed and killed there.

5 A whale or sharks might even have overturned the boat!

One, or all of them, went mad.

1 They drank some of the commercial alcohol. There was a fight. Some were killed, the others left. (But commercial alcohol is very poisonous.)

2 The cook was crazy and poisoned everybody. Then he killed himself after throwing the bodies into the sea.

3 The captain had an attack of religious mania, killed everybody, then himself.

4 There was a fungus called 'ergot' in the bread. This is a fungus which can grow on rye bread. It is very similar to the drug LSD. Whole villages had been poisoned in this way in medieval Europe.

Crime.

1 The 'Dei Gratia' attacked the 'Mary Celeste' and killed everybody.

2 Pirates attacked and killed them.

3 There was a mutiny (a revolution against the captain of a ship). Two of the crew were criminals. There was a fight. Some were killed. The others left.

4 Mrs Briggs fell in love with one of the crew. Again there was a fight.

5 The crew of the 'Mary Celeste' attacked and robbed another ship, and left on the other ship with its cargo. (Which other ship? There are no records.)

6 They found an abandoned ship with a valuable cargo, and stole it.

7 Captain Briggs and Captain Moorhouse planned everything together, for the salvage money. The ship was never abandoned. None of the story was true.

Outside forces.

1 A spaceship from another planet took everybody away.

2 A giant wave knocked them all from the deck, or a tornado.

3 A sea monster (a giant octopus or sea serpent) attacked the ship.

4 Men living below the sea attacked the ship, when it passed over the old site of Atlantis.

SPECULATION

1△

Look at this

| He
She
They
It | must
could
may
might
might even
can't
couldn't | be
have been | crazy.
at home. |
| | | be doing
have done
have been
doing | something. |

Make as many sentences as possible about each of the pictures.

2△

3△

4△

5△

6△

7△

8△

9△

11△

10
◁

12△

Unit 30

APOLOGIES

C Excuse me.
D Yes?
C Would you mind putting out your cigarette?
D I beg your pardon?
C This is a 'no smoking' compartment!
D Is it? I didn't see a sign.
C There it is. On the window.
D Oh, yes. I'm terribly sorry.

G Oi! You!
H Me?
G Yes, you. What do you think you're doing?
H Pardon? I'm just waiting for the bus.
G Well, there's a queue, you know.
H Is there? Sorry ... I didn't mean to push in. I didn't realize there was a queue.

A Hello. Derek Moore speaking.
B Oh, hello, Derek. This is Clive.
A Ah, yes. Did you get home all right?
B Yes, thanks, but I just wanted to apologize for last night.
A Don't worry about it. It really doesn't matter.
B But the carpet, it must be ruined. It was so silly of me to put the cup on the floor.
A Forget it, Clive. It's all right now.
B But it must have made an awful stain.
A Look, it's nothing. I was annoyed last night, but it doesn't look so bad this morning.
B Anyway, you must let me pay for the cleaning.
A Listen, Clive. Accidents happen. They always do at parties. I don't want to hear any more about it. Right?
B All right. I really am very sorry.
A See you on Monday. Bye.

E Oh! Good morning, Mrs New-bury.
F Good afternoon, Sharon. Late again?
E Oh, yes. I'm ever so sorry. I couldn't find a parking place.
F Perhaps you should have left home earlier.
E Yes, I know. It won't happen again.
F It'd better not, Sharon. This is the third time this week!

I Are you OK?
J Yes, I'm all right, but what about my car?
I There's not too much damage.
J What! Just look at it! I only bought it last week. You shouldn't have been going so fast.
I Well, I'm sorry, but it wasn't my fault.
J Wasn't your fault? What do you mean? I had right of way.
I I'm afraid you didn't. You shouldn't have come out like that.
J Why not? There's no sign.
I What's that there then?
J Oh, yes. A 'stop' sign. I must have missed it.
I Well, you should be more careful. You could have killed us all!
J Yes ... I'm sorry. What more can I say?
I All right ... all right. At least no-body's hurt. Here come the police. You'd better explain it to them.

THEY DIDN'T STOP TO TELL ME!

LORRY HIJACKINGS ON THE INCREASE

The Road Transport Industry is becoming increasingly concerned about the number of lorry hijackings.

The hijackers seem to be both well-organized and well-informed. The gangs concentrate on trucks carrying high-value marketable loads, for example cigarettes, alcohol, or electrical goods. Drivers have now been forbidden to pick up hitch-hikers, and have been warned to take extra care when parking in motorway service areas. Yesterday's hijacking at Burnham Wood on the M6 was the fourth in the area this month.

Inspector Waterman is interviewing Stan Fletcher, the driver of the hijacked truck.

Inspector Sit down, Mr Fletcher. Cigarette?

Stan No, thanks. I'm trying to stop smoking.

Inspector Now, Mr Fletcher. How did you manage to lose your truck?

Stan You know the story already.

Inspector Well, tell us again.

Stan OK. I was driving down the M6 from Scotland carrying whisky ... in cases.

Inspector Hmm.

Stan I decided to stop at Burnham Wood.

Inspector Why Burnham Wood?

Stan I stopped to get some diesel and I needed a coffee. I'd been driving for three hours.

Inspector Go on.

Stan After I'd filled the tank, I parked outside the café.

Inspector Yes.

Stan I got my coffee and sat by the window to keep an eye on the truck.

Inspector Did you see anybody near the lorry?

Stan No, nobody. Then I went to make a phone call.

Inspector A phone call?

Stan Yes, you can check. I stopped to get some change at the cash desk.

Inspector OK. Then?

Stan Well, I was talking to my wife on the phone when I saw the lorry going past the window. I couldn't believe my eyes. I dropped the phone and ran outside ... but it was too late!

Inspector Had you remembered to lock the cab door?

Stan Yes, I always remember to lock it. I'm not stupid, you know!

Inspector All right. All right. But can you actually remember locking it on this occasion?

Stan Yes, definitely.

Inspector How can you be so sure?

Stan Well, I remember putting the key in the lock. It was all wet and dirty. It was raining, you see, and I'd dropped it in a puddle.

Inspector And the passenger door? Did you remember to check that?

Stan I don't actually remember checking it. But I'm sure I must have done. It locks from the inside, and I never use that door.

Inspector But you don't remember checking it?

Stan No, not really. But you can't remember everything, can you? I might've forgotten to check it.

Inspector So it could've been open.

Stan Yes ... yes, it could've been. But I bet it wasn't!

Inspector Well, what's your theory, Mr Fletcher?

Stan They must've had keys, mustn't they? They started the engine, didn't they?

Inspector How did they get the keys?

Stan Don't ask me. I've got no idea. They didn't stop to tell me!

Look at this

He was driving. He stopped. He got some petrol.

A *What did he stop doing? He stopped driving.*

B *What did he stop to do? He stopped to get some petrol.*

Exercise 1

Now make questions and answers from these sentences.

1 He was driving. He stopped. He had a cup of coffee.

2 He was watching the truck. He stopped. He made a phone call.

3 He was talking to his wife. He stopped. He ran outside.

Look at this

I proposed to my wife on the beach at sunset. I can see it now!
I remember proposing to my wife.

I was told to post this letter. I've still got it.
I didn't remember to post it.
I forgot to post it.

Exercise 2

Make sentences.

1 I should have closed the window, but it's still open.

2 I once met the Queen. I can remember it very clearly.

3 There's a film on television. I saw it at the cinema ten years ago.

4 He ought to have done his homework. The teacher's very angry.

Unit 33

JOHN LENNON 1940-1980

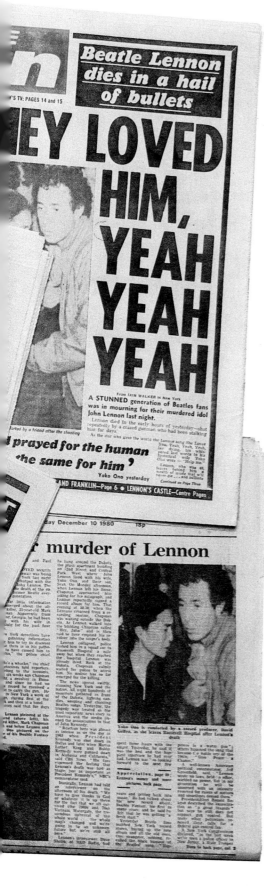

John Lennon was murdered just before 11 pm on the 8th December 1980 outside his home in the Dakota Apartment Building in New York City. He had just got out of a car, and was walking to the entrance when a voice called 'Mr Lennon'. Lennon turned, and was shot five times. The killer threw his gun down, and stood there smiling. 'Do you know what you just did?' shouted the doorman. 'I just shot John Lennon,' the killer replied. Lennon was rushed to hospital in a police patrol car, but it was too late. The killer was 25 year-old Mark Chapman from Hawaii. Earlier the same evening he had asked Lennon for his autograph. In fact, he had been hanging around outside the apartment building for several days. Chapman was a fan of the Beatles and Lennon, and had tried to imitate him in many ways. It is said that he even believed that he was John Lennon.

Biographical notes

1940 Born Liverpool
1942 Lennon family deserted by father. Mother leaves. John brought up by aunt.
1956 Forms pop group at school.
1957 Student at Liverpool College of Art.
1958 Mother killed in road accident.
1960 Goes professional as one of 'The Beatles' (Lennon, McCartney, Harrison, Best, Sutcliffe). Plays in Hamburg, Germany.
1961 Plays in Hamburg and Liverpool. Sutcliffe (Lennon's best friend) dies of a brain tumour. Brian Epstein begins to manage the Beatles.
1962 Ringo Starr replaces Pete Best as Beatles drummer. Married Cynthia Powell, an art student. Beatles' first record 'Love me do'. First TV appearance.

1963 Three records Number 1 in British Top 20. Incredible popularity. Son, Julian, born.
1964 First hit record in USA 'I want to hold your hand'. Two US tours. In April, Beatles records at Number 1, 2, 3, 4, and 5 in US Top 20. First film 'A Hard Day's Night'. First book.
1965 'Help!' Beatles' second film. Beatlemania at its height. US tour. Huge audiences in football stadiums. Beatles receive MBE (special honorary award) from Queen Elizabeth.

1966 Lennon in film 'How I won the War' – not a musical. Meets Yoko Ono, Japanese avant-garde artist.
1967 'Sergeant Pepper' – Beatles' most famous LP. All the Beatles interested in meditation. Manager Brian Epstein found dead from sleeping-pill overdose.
1968 In India with Beatles for meditation. Beatles' company 'Apple' founded. Lennon art exhibition 'You are here'. Lennon divorced by wife.
1969 Beatles' film 'Let it Be'. Rumours of quarrels about money. Talk of Beatles' break up. Beatles' last performance on roof of Apple Building. Lennon and Yoko Ono marry. He 29. She 36. Lennon still recording with Beatles but some work solo.

1970 McCartney leaves Beatles. Others start solo careers.
1971 Lennon LP 'Imagine' – most successful LP. Lennon and Yoko Ono in New York one-room apartment.
1972 Charity concerts.
1973 Lennon and Yoko Ono separate. Lennon in Los Angeles. Lennon ordered to leave USA – protests and appeals.
1974 Drink problem – one and a half bottles of spirits a day. Still fighting deportation.
1975 Lennon and Yoko Ono together again in New York. Permission to stay in USA. Son Sean born October 9th (Lennon's birthday).
1976 Retires from public life. Extensive travel. Business affairs managed by Yoko Ono.
1976 –80 Full-time father. Very close relationship with son. Owns seven apartments in same block – one as a cold-store for fur coats.
1980 First record for six years. LP 'Double Fantasy'. Single 'Starting Over'. Good reviews from critics. Many said it was 'a new beginning'. Dec 8th Lennon murdered. Massive media coverage. TV and radio programmes interrupted to give news. Record companies on overtime to produce records.
1981 In January and February three records at Number 1 in British Top 20: '(Just Like) Starting Over', 'Imagine' and 'Woman'.

KIDNAPPED

Hugh Rolan is a wealthy business-man. His wife phoned him an hour ago to tell him that their daughter hadn't returned home from school. He told her not to worry and came home at once. He's just arrived to find his wife in tears.

Hugh Pamela, what's wrong? Is it Caroline?

Pamela Yes. This note came through the door. She ... she ... she's been kidnapped!

Hugh Kidnapped! Oh, my God, no! Have you phoned the police?

Pamela No, no. Don't touch the phone! Read the note first.

Hugh Half a million pounds! It'll take me a few days to get that much cash together.

Pamela How long?

Hugh I don't know. I just can't put my hands on that much money. Not immediately. Maybe we should phone the police.

Pamela No, not the police! If the kidnappers find out, they'll kill her.

Hugh But I'll have to borrow the money. If I don't tell the police, the bank won't let me have it.

Pamela Oh, Hugh! Unless we do exactly what they say, we may never see her again.

Hugh Hugh Rolan.

Voice Did you get our note?

Hugh Yes.

Voice Have you told the police?

Hugh No ... not yet.

Voice You'd better not. When can you get the money?

Hugh I need a few days.

Voice You've got one day.

Hugh How do we know that Caroline is still alive?

Voice You don't. You'll have to trust us. Get the money by tomorrow evening. You'll hear from us again.

Hugh If you harm a hair on her head, I'll ... I'll ...

We have got your **daughter**
She is safe and well
We want **£500,000** If you
give us the **money** she will be **OK**
don't phone the **POLICE** or we'll
KILL her If you **try** to
contact them, **We'll** know
If you **don't** follow our **INSTRUCTIONS**
your **daughter** will **DIE** UNLESS
you pay up you'll **never** **see** her again.

Exercise 1

1 If you were Hugh, would you tele-phone the police?
2 If you were the kidnappers, how would you arrange to get the money?
3 If you were Hugh and Pamela, what would you do?
4 If you were the police, what would you do?

Exercise 2

A *Give me the money!*
B *Why?*
A *If you don't give me the money, I'll kill you.*
B *What? You're joking!*
A *No, I'm not. Unless you give me the money, I'll kill you.*

Now look at the pictures, and make similar conversations.

Exercise 3

Look at Exercise 2.
What would you do in these situations?
If I were him, I'd give him the money.
If I were him, I'd run away.
If I were him, I'd hit the robber with the briefcase.

HAVE YOU SEEN THIS ADVERT?

Stephen Wendy, have you seen this advert?

Wendy Mmm. It looks great, doesn't it? I phoned them an hour ago. They'll ring me back if they want me.

Stephen Oh, they'll want you. I mean you've got beautiful long hair.

Wendy I hope so! If I go, I'll get a new hairstyle ... and a day out in London.

Louise Colin, take a look at this.

Colin Oh, yes, I've seen it. I'm going to phone tomorrow.

Louise It sounds very exciting, and you've got a decent car.

Colin Hmm. There are some disadvantages.

Louise Every job's got disadvantages, but you're always complaining about your present job.

Colin I know. I'm prepared to try it. But we haven't got a phone. I won't take it if they don't pay the phone bills!

Rachel Helen, what do you think of this advertisement?

Helen Didn't I tell you? It was in last week's paper too. I applied. I've got an interview tomorrow.

Rachel Do you think you'll get it?

Helen They seemed very keen on the phone. I think they'll offer me the job.

Rachel So, you're going to California!

Helen I didn't say that. I won't take the job unless they agree to pay my return fare. It'll be hard work with five kids, and I won't go unless they offer me a good salary!

Look at this

I'm interested. I've applied.	I'm not interested. I haven't applied.
If they offer enough money, I'll accept the job.	If they offered more money, I'd apply.
If they don't pay more, I won't accept the job.	If they didn't offer enough, I wouldn't accept the job.
Unless they pay more, I won't accept the job.	Unless they offered more, I wouldn't accept the job.

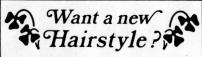

Want a new Hairstyle?

Volunteer models required for national hairstyling competition.

Wednesday 28th January
Carlton Towers Hotel, London

* Free dinner
* Rail fares paid

Only qualification needed is long hair (at least 20 cm)

 Tel: 01-129 7880

ARE YOU AMBITIOUS?

– are you aged 22–35?
– do you need a challenge?
– tired of your present job?

Some of our sales representatives earn more than the Prime Minister!!!

All you need is energy, enthusiasm, and your own car and telephone. No salary. Commission only basis.

Contact: **DIRECT SALES LTD.**, Suite 34, Plaza Hotel, Liverpool   051-174 2330

ARE YOU FOND OF CHILDREN?

Nanny wanted for British family living in L.A., California, with 5 children aged between 1 and 8. Must have driving licence. Own room/bathroom. One way air fare paid. Two weeks holiday a year. Tuesday evenings free. Salary negotiable.

Write to BOX NO. 3/646.

Mandy Hey, Andrew. Look at this ad.

Andrew It looks fun. Why don't you ring?

Mandy I'd love to, but it's a waste of time. My hair's far too short.

Andrew Well, I like it the way it is. Anyway, you don't know what they might do. Blue and green hair's fashionable at the moment.

Mandy Oh, Andrew, I wouldn't mind that. If I had longer hair, I'd phone them.

Roger Sandra, did you see this?

Sandra Yes. You aren't interested, are you?

Roger What? Me? I wasn't born yesterday! There are far too many things wrong with it.

Sandra What do you mean?

Roger I wouldn't take a job like that! You wouldn't have any security. You wouldn't earn anything if you didn't work all day, every day. And I wouldn't take a sales job if they didn't provide a car.

Sandra Yes, look at the address. It's a hotel room. I certainly wouldn't work for a company if they didn't even have an office!

Jane There's a job in America in the paper.

Tina Yes, I know. I wouldn't dream of applying for it.

Jane Why not? You've been looking for a job in the States.

Tina It's slave labour, isn't it? Five kids, and one evening off a week.

Jane But the money might be very good.

Tina Huh! I wouldn't take it unless they paid me a really good salary with longer holidays and more free time. And I certainly wouldn't go anywhere abroad unless they paid my return fare!

Exercise

Could you ever kill a person?
Not unless they tried to kill me.
I wouldn't do it unless they tried to kill me.
What about these things?
Would you ever steal food?/rob a bank?/hit someone?/eat a cat?/jump from a high building?/take your clothes off in the street?/jump with a parachute?/have a heart transplant?

'Good evening, and welcome again to the 'Michael Parkhurst Talkabout'. In tonight's programme, we're looking at the problem of energy. The world's energy resources are limited. Nobody knows exactly how much fuel is left, but pessimistic forecasts say that there is only enough coal for 450 years, enough natural gas for 50 years and that oil might run out in 30 years. Obviously we have to do something, and we have to do it soon!

I'd like to welcome our first guest, Professor Marvin Burnham of the New England Institute of Technology. Professor Burnham.'

'Well, we are in an energy crisis and we will have to do something quickly. Fossil fuels (coal, oil and gas) are rapidly running out. The tragedy is that fossil fuels are far too valuable to waste on the production of electricity. Just think of all the things you can make from oil! If we don't start conserving these things now, it will be too late. And nuclear power is the only real alternative. We are getting some electricity from nuclear power-stations already. If we invest in further research now, we'll be ready to face the future. There's been a lot of protest lately against nuclear power – some people will protest at anything – but nuclear power-stations are not as dangerous as some people say. It's far more dangerous to work down a coal-mine or on a North Sea oil-rig. Safety regulations in power-stations are very strict.

If we spent money on research now, we could develop stations which create their own fuel and burn their own waste. In many parts of the world where there are no fossil fuels, nuclear power is the only alternative. If you accept that we need electricity, then we will need nuclear energy. Just imagine what the world would be like if we didn't have electricity – no heating, no lighting, no transport, no radio or TV. Just think about the ways you use electricity every day. Surely we don't want to go back to the Stone Age. That's what will happen if we turn our backs on nuclear research.'

'Thank you, Professor. Our next guest is a member of CANE, the Campaign Against Nuclear Energy, Jennifer Hughes.'

'Right. I must disagree totally with Professor Burnham. Let's look at the facts. First, there is no perfect machine. I mean, why do aeroplanes

ENERGY CRISIS

crash? Machines fail. People make mistakes. What would happen if there were a serious nuclear accident? And an accident must be inevitable – sooner or later. Huge areas would be evacuated, and they could remain contaminated with radioactivity for years. If it happened in your area, you wouldn't get a penny in compensation. No insurance company covers nuclear risks. There are accidents. If the nuclear industry didn't keep them quiet, there would be a public outcry. Radioactivity causes cancer and may affect future generations.

Next, nuclear waste. There is no technology for absolutely safe disposal. Some of this waste will remain active for thousands of years. Is that what you want to leave to your children? And their children's children? A reactor only lasts about 25 years. By the year 2000 we'll have 'retired' 26 reactors in the UK.

Next, terrorism. Terrorists could hold the nation to ransom if they captured a reactor. In the USA the Savannah River plant, and Professor Burnham knows this very well, lost (yes, 'lost') enough plutonium ·be-

tween 1955 and 1978 to make 18 (18!) atom bombs. Where is it? Who's got it? I consider that nuclear energy is expensive, dangerous, and evil, and most of all, absolutely unnecessary. But Dr Woodstock will be saying more about that.'

'Thank you Jennifer. Now I'm very pleased to welcome Dr Catherine Woodstock. She is the author of several books on alternative technology.'

'Hello. I'd like to begin by agreeing with Jennifer. We can develop alternative sources of power, and unless we try we'll never succeed. Instead of burning fossil fuels we should be concentrating on more economic uses of electricity, because electricity can be produced from any source of energy. If we didn't waste so much energy, our resources would last longer. You can save more energy by conservation than you can produce for the same money. Unless we do research on solar energy, wind power, wave power, tidal power, hydroelectric schemes etc, our fossil fuels will run out, and we'll all freeze or starve to death. Other countries are spending much more than us on research, and don't forget that energy from the sun, the waves and the wind lasts for ever. We really won't survive unless we start working on cleaner, safer sources of energy.'

'Thank you very much, Dr Woodstock. Our final speaker, before we open the discussion to the studio audience, is Charles Wicks, MP, the Minister for Energy.'

'I've been listening to the other speakers with great interest. By the way, I don't agree with some of the estimates of world energy reserves. More oil and gas is being discovered all the time. If we listened to the pessimists (and there are a lot of them about) none of us would sleep at night. In the short-term, we must continue to rely on the fossil fuels – oil, coal and gas. But we must also look to the future. Our policy must be flexible. Unless we thought new research was necessary, we wouldn't be spending money on it. After all, the Government wouldn't have a Department of Energy unless they thought it was important. The big question is where to spend the money – on conservation of present resources or on research into new forms of power. But I'm fairly optimistic. I wouldn't be in this job unless I were an optimist!'

Unit 36

WHAT WOULD YOU HAVE DONE?

YOUR LETTERS

What would you have done?

Last week we invited readers to write and tell us about things that had happened to them, or things that they had heard about. We wanted stories where people just didn't know what to do next! Here are the stories that interested us most!

That's my beer . . . that was!

I was in a small country pub. I had just sat down with a pint of beer. Suddenly this huge man – he looked like a boxer – came over, picked up my beer, drank it, banged the glass down on the table, stared at me, and then walked away without saying anything. I suppose I should have said something, but I was scared stiff! I didn't know what to do! What would you have done?

Mr A Watney, Hull.

In deep water

I was on a touring holiday in France. It was a very hot day and I stopped at a small deserted beach. I hadn't got my swimming-costume with me, but it was early in the morning and there were no people or houses in sight. So I took off all my clothes and swam out to sea. I'm a very strong swimmer. I lay on my back, closed my eyes, and relaxed in the water. When I looked back at the beach, a coach had arrived and there were thirty or forty people sitting on the sand having a picnic! What would you have done?

Mr T Horniman, Ipswich.

Naughty Bishop!

I was told a lovely story about the Bishop of Fleetwood.

He'd gone to New York for a church conference. Anyway, when he stepped off the plane there were a lot of journalists and cameramen. The first question one of the journalists asked was 'Do you intend to visit any nightclubs in New York?' Well, the Bishop was 85 years old. 'Are there any nightclubs in New York?' he answered innocently. The next morning the headline in one of the New York papers was 'Bishop's first question on arrival in New York – Are there any nightclubs?' How would you have felt?

Reverend Simon Fisher, Exeter.

Strangers in the night

My story isn't at all funny. It was a very frightening experience. You see, one night I woke up suddenly. I heard the tinkle of broken glass from downstairs, and I heard the window opening. Then I heard two voices! My wife had woken up, too. She told me to do something. A couple of days before, there had been a report about a burglary in the local paper. The burglars had been interrupted and they had beaten up the householder. They'd nearly killed him. I was trembling with fear. I just didn't know what to do. In the end, I didn't go down and they stole the silver tea-service I'd inherited from my mother. Was I right? What would you have done?

Mr D Boswell, Edinburgh.

A saucy thief

I had parked my car in a multi-storey car park and I was taking a short cut through the side door of the restaurant in a large store. Half-way across the restaurant I spotted my father eating pie, chips and peas – he often eats there. I crept up behind him, put my hand over his shoulder, took a chip off the plate, dipped it in the tomato sauce and ate it. Then I realized that the man was not my father! I was so embarrassed! I couldn't say a word! What would you have done?

Miss H P Branston, Cardiff.

Unless!!!

I'd just parked my car in the street near a football stadium in Liverpool. It was ten minutes before the start of the match and I was in a hurry. Two little boys came up to me and said 'Give us 50p and we'll look after your car while you're at the match.' I told them to clear off, and one of them looked at me with big, round, innocent eyes and said 'Unless you give us the money, something might happen to your car while you're away. You know, a scratch or a flat tyre. Something like that.' I was furious! What would you have done!

Mr D Revie, Birkenhead.

Honesty is the best policy

I couldn't believe a story I heard the other day. It seems that a couple had just bought a house in Manchester. They wanted to insulate the roof, so they climbed up into the loft. There, under the water tank, was £20,000 in cash! They handed over the money to the police. Would you have reported the find? What would you have done?

Mrs B Leyland, Birmingham.

Look at this

Would you have said anything?
What would you have done?

I	'd		have	said	something.
	would			done	
	wouldn't				anything.

Exercise 1
Make sentences like this about each of the seven stories.

Exercise 2
Tell the story of an interesting, surprising or embarrassing experience you have had, or heard about.

A BAD DAY AT THE OFFICE

Bob What was wrong with you this morning?

Debbie Wrong with me? Sorry, Bob, I don't know what you mean.

Bob You walked straight past me. You didn't say a word!

Debbie Really? Where?

Bob It was just outside the newsagent's in the High Street.

Debbie I'm terribly sorry, Bob. I just didn't see you.

Bob Come on, Debbie. You must have done! I was waving!

Debbie No, honestly. I didn't see you. If I had seen you, I would have said 'Hello'.

Exercise 1
She didn't see him. She didn't say 'Hello'.
If she had seen him, she would have said 'Hello'.
Do the same.
1 She didn't notice him. She didn't stop.
2 She didn't recognize him. She didn't speak to him.
3 She didn't see him waving. She didn't wave back.

Mrs Lewis Debbie, have you sent that telex to Geneva?

Debbie No, I haven't.

Mrs Lewis Why haven't you done it yet? It's urgent.

Debbie Because you didn't ask me to do it.

Mrs Lewis Didn't I?

Debbie No, you didn't. If you'd asked me, I'd've sent it!

Exercise 2
Have you sent the telex?
If you'd asked me, I would have sent it.
Do the same.
1 Have you posted the letters?
2 Have you photo-copied the report?
3 Have you typed the contract?

Gordon Did you see a letter from Brazil on this desk?

Debbie Yes, it's here.

Gordon Oh, good. Where's the envelope?

Debbie I threw it away. Why?

Gordon It had some nice stamps on it. I wanted them for my son. He collects stamps.

Debbie Oh, Gordon! If only I'd known!

Gordon It doesn't matter.

Debbie No, I'd have kept it if I'd known.

Exercise 3
I didn't keep it.
I'd have kept it if I'd known.
Do the same.
1 I didn't do it.
2 I didn't give it to you.
3 I didn't put it in the drawer.

Debbie What's the matter, Jeff? You don't look very well.

Jeff No. I've had a terrible cold. I've been in bed all weekend, but it's better today.

Debbie Mm ... I had a bad cold last week.

Jeff I know, and you gave it to everyone in the office. I wouldn't have come to work if I'd had a cold like that.

Exercise 4
She had a bad cold, but she came to work.
I wouldn't have come to work if I'd had a cold.
Do the same.
1 She had a headache. She stayed at work.

2 He had a sore throat. He worked all day.
3 She had toothache. She didn't go to the dentist.

Mrs Lewis Debbie.

Debbie Yes.

Mrs Lewis Did you type this letter?

Debbie Yes. Why? Is there something wrong with it?

Mrs Lewis Have a look. This should be £400.00. You've typed £40,000.

Debbie Oh, yes. I'm ever so sorry.

Mrs Lewis And you've also misspelt the customer's name. It should be 'Snelling' not 'Smelling'.

Debbie Hee-hee!

Mrs Lewis It's not funny, Debbie. If I hadn't noticed it, we could have lost the order.

Exercise 5
She noticed the error. They didn't lose the order.
If she hadn't noticed the error, they could have lost the order.
Do the same.
1 She noticed the spelling mistake. They didn't upset the customer.
2 She saw it in time. They didn't send the letter.
3 She checked the letter. They didn't post it.

Ruth Hi, Debbie. Did you have a good day, today?

Debbie No, I didn't. I'm glad today's over! Everything went wrong!

Ruth Really?

Debbie Yes, I made a lot of typing errors, then I forgot to send a telex and I offended Bob because I ignored him in the street.

Ruth Why was that?

Debbie It was that party last night. If I hadn't gone to bed late, it wouldn't have been such an awful day. I'm having an early night tonight!

Exercise 6
I went to a party./I went to bed late./I forgot to set the alarm./I got up late./I missed the bus./I was late for work./I've had a bad day./I forgot to send a telex./I made a typing error.
If I hadn't gone to the party, none of these things would have happened.
If I hadn't gone to a party, I wouldn't have gone to bed late.
Make eight sentences.

A SATURDAY AFTERNOON

Gillian felt slightly uneasy as the porter unlocked the gates and waved her through. St Alfred's Hospital was not an ordinary mental institution. It was the most exclusive institution of its type in the country. You had to be not only mentally ill, but also extremely wealthy to be accepted as a patient. She parked her car outside the main entrance of the imposing eighteenth century building. She paused on the steps to look at the superb ornamental gardens and surrounding parkland. An old man in a white panama hat was watering the flowerbed beside the steps. He smiled at her.

Old man Good afternoon, miss. A lovely day, isn't it?

Gillian Yes, it certainly is.

Old man Are you a new patient?

Gillian Oh, I'm not a patient. I'm just here to do some research.

Old man Will you be staying long?

Gillian I really don't know. I wonder if you could direct me to Dr Carmichael's office?

Old man Certainly, miss. Just go through the main door, turn left, walk down to the end of the corridor, and it's the last door on the right.

Gillian Thank you very much indeed.

Dr Carmichael was waiting for her. He had been looking forward to meeting his new research assistant. He himself had always been interested in the special problems of long-stay patients. Dr Carmichael was very proud of his hospital and she was impressed by the relaxed and informal atmosphere. She spent the mornings interviewing patients, and the afternoons writing up the results of her research in the gardens. Some of the patients were withdrawn and depressed, some seemed almost normal. Only one or two had to be kept locked up. She found it hard to believe that all of them had been thought too dangerous to live in normal society. She often saw the old man in the panama hat. He spent most of his time working in the gardens, but he always stopped to speak to her. She found out that his name was Maurice Featherstone. He was a gentle and mild-mannered old fellow,

with clear, blue, honest eyes, white hair and a pinkish complexion. He always looked pleased with life. She became particularly curious about him, but Dr Carmichael had never asked her to interview him, and she wondered why. One night, at dinner, she asked about Mr Featherstone.

Dr Carmichael Ah, yes, Maurice. Nice old chap. He's been here longer than anybody.

Gillian What's wrong with him?

Dr Carmichael Nothing. His family put him here thirty-five years ago. They never come to visit him, but the bills are always paid on time.

Gillian But what had he done?

Dr Carmichael I'll show you his file. It seems that he burnt down his school when he was seventeen. His family tried to keep the incident quiet. Over the next few years there were a number of mysterious fires in his neighbourhood, but the family did nothing until he tried to set fire to the family mansion. He was in here the next day. Maurice never protested.

Gillian And that was thirty-five years ago!

Dr Carmichael I'm afraid so. If I'd had my way, I'd have let him out years ago.

Gillian But he can't still be dangerous!

Dr Carmichael No. He's had plenty of opportunities. We even let him smoke. If he'd wanted to start a fire, he could have done it at any time.

Gillian was shocked by the story. She became determined to do something about it. She wrote letters to Maurice's family, but never received a reply. He had never been officially certified as insane, and legally, he could leave at any time. Dr Carmichael was easily persuaded to let her talk to Maurice.

Gillian Maurice, have you ever thought about leaving this place?

Maurice No, miss. I'm very happy here. This is my home. And anyway, I've got nowhere to go.

Gillian But wouldn't you like to go into the village sometimes ... to walk around, to buy your own tobacco?

Maurice I've never thought about it, miss. I suppose it would be nice. But I wouldn't want to stay away for long. I've spent twenty years working on this garden. I know every flower and tree. What would happen to them if I weren't here?

Gillian realized that it would be unkind to make him leave the hospital. However, she found out that the next Saturday was his birthday. She arranged with the staff to give him a party. They wanted it to be a surprise and Dr Carmichael agreed to let him go out for the afternoon. There was a flower show in the village. Maurice left at two o'clock. He seemed quite excited. They expected him to return about four o'clock. The cook had made a birthday cake and the staff had decorated the lounge.

Gillian was standing in the window when she saw him. He was early. He was walking up the drive towards the house, whistling cheerfully. Behind him, above the trees, several thick black columns of smoke were beginning to rise slowly into the clear blue sky.

Transatlantic Airways
The Golden West 14 days   San Francisco 6 nights   Las Vegas 2 nights   Los Angeles 6 nights

Can you see yourself riding a cable-car in San Francisco, eating fresh crab and lobster at Fisherman's Wharf, winning a fortune in the casinos of Las Vegas or walking with the stars along Hollywood Boulevard? Transatlantic Airways invite you to spend two unforgettable weeks in the cities of California and Nevada and enjoy the glitter and the glamour of the Golden West.

Every city has it own character – San Francisco with the Golden Gate Bridge, Chinatown, cable-cars climbing up the steep hills, restaurants serving food from every country in the world. You'll be offered tours to see the scenery of Monterey and Carmel, and the breathtaking views from the Pacific Coast Highway.

Then you join in the razzamatazz of Las Vegas, the gambling capital of the world, set in the Nevada Desert. Las Vegas never sleeps and the entertainment is the finest in the world. And from Las Vegas there's an optional flight over the spectacular Grand Canyon.

Finally you arrive in Los Angeles, home of the movie industry. Sunset Strip, Beverly Hills and Hollywood all wait to welcome you. You'll be able to choose any number of excursions – the wonderful world of Disneyland, Universal Film Studios or even a shopping trip to Mexico.

This exciting three-centre tour offers you a golden opportunity to experience the special atmosphere of the Golden West.

HOLIDAY USA

Mark and Emma Austin are a young couple in their late twenties. Emma was interviewed about the holiday.

'On the whole we enjoyed it very much, but it was pretty tiring. We went on most of the excursions, because we didn't want to miss anything. We really felt we needed more time. If we went again, we'd stay longer. We would have spent more time in San Francisco and less time in Los Angeles if we'd known more about the cities. Los Angeles was a bit disappointing. We went on a tour of Beverly Hills to see the 'houses of the stars'. Unless you'd studied film history, you would never have heard of most of them! Generally speaking, the hotels, food and service were excellent. We found Americans particularly friendly. We probably took too much luggage. Clothes in the States were so cheap! It would have been a good idea to take empty suitcases! If we'd done that, the savings on clothes would almost have paid for the air fare!'

Jack and Vera Drake are a retired couple. Jack was asked about the holiday.

'We'd been looking forward to this trip for years, and it was the holiday of a lifetime. I think we liked Las Vegas most, but two nights were probably enough! If we'd stayed there much longer, we'd have lost all our money! We saw Tom Jones at the Desert Inn. I've never seen anything like that place! Disneyland is a 'must' for anyone with children. If only we'd had our grandchildren with us! They would have loved it! We went on some of the excursions, and we could have gone on more, but you can't see everything, can you? I didn't think much of American beer, but Californian wine was a nice surprise. We wouldn't have chosen this tour unless it had been escorted. We're both in our seventies and we couldn't have managed on our own. Everybody was so helpful to us!'

HOLIDAY USA

Fly-drive means freedom – the freedom of the road to explore this exciting country. Fly-drive must be the logical way of seeing the land of the motel and the freeway. America is made for drivers. American cars are easy to drive, comfortable, and petrol is much cheaper than in Europe. A flexible timetable is the ideal way of getting the most out of your holiday. We book your first night's accommodation in a hotel near the airport and deliver your car in the morning. Then you are as free as a bird – go anywhere, stay anywhere. If you wish to pre-pay your accommodation before departure, we can supply accommodation vouchers for one of the large chain of motels.

Boston is the ideal starting-point to explore New England. To the southeast are the rocky cliffs and sandy beaches of beautiful Cape Cod, ideal for swimming, sailing and fishing. To the north is New Hampshire with its green valleys, white steepled churches and infinite variety of wild flowers. Drive up into Maine, a land of forests and mountains with a spectacular coastline. Drive west across New York State to Niagara Falls or south through the beautiful rolling hills of Connecticut to a coastline of resort towns and fishing ports.

Matthew and Polly Winthrop took their two children on the fly-drive holiday. Polly's talking about it.

'We'd never have gone fly-drive unless we'd had the kids with us. Matthew is a bus-driver and it wasn't much of a holiday for him! But I think it's the only way to travel with young children. The distances were much greater than we had imagined. If we had another holiday in the States, we wouldn't try to drive so far. I think we'd cover the longer distances by plane, and then hire a different car in each place. The motels were very well equipped and the children were always made welcome. The motels didn't have much character, but when you're touring you just need somewhere to sleep. Every room had TV; for us that was marvellous. We wouldn't have been able to leave the children if there hadn't been a TV in the room. We would never have left them alone for too long of course, but it was nice for us to go down to the bar for a drink. New England was absolutely fantastic and we'd recommend it to anyone!'

Ian and Chris are in their early twenties. Chris spoke about their holiday.

'It was really great. We took it in turns to drive, so the distances didn't seem too long. American cars are tremendous. They're so big. One night we couldn't find a motel, and we slept in the car. We bought loads of records and clothes. If we'd bought them in England, they'd have cost twice as much. We went in the autumn, they'd call it 'fall' in the States, and the colours on the trees in New England were unbelievable! We wouldn't have chosen this holiday unless we'd liked driving. You spend a lot of time in the car. We intend to go again next year, but we'll go to Miami or San Francisco, if we can afford it!'

Unit 40

FOOD FOR THOUGHT

"One man's meat is another man's poison."
English proverb.

There is a wide range of nutritious foods in the world. However, eating habits differ from country to country. In some societies certain foods are taboo. An eccentric millionaire once invited guests from several countries to a banquet and offered them this menu. All the foods are popular in some parts of the world, but are not eaten in others.

STARTERS	
Snails	100-year-old eggs
Frogs' legs	Tripe (cow's stomach)
Pigs' feet	Black pudding (made from
Shellfish	blood)
Caviare	

SOUPS
Bird's nest soup
Shark fin soup
Sea-weed soup

FISH
Octopus
Jellied eels

MAIN COURSES	
Brains	Whale
Whole stuffed camel	Roast dog
Grilled songbirds	Pork
Roast snake	Beef
Bat stew	Lamb
Horsemeat	Veal
Kangaroo	

DESSERT
Chocolate-covered ants
Salad of flower petals

If you had been there, which items could you have eaten? Which items would you have eaten? Which items couldn't you have eaten? Why not?

Do you know which countries they are popular in? Would you eat them, if you were starving?

What unusual things are eaten in your country? Has your country got a national dish? How do you make it?

"Part of the secret of success in life is to eat what you like, and let the food fight it out inside you."
Mark Twain.

Here are some common ideas about food: Eating carrots is good for the eyes.
Fish is good for the brain.
Eating cheese at night makes you dream.
Garlic stops you getting colds.
Drinking coffee stops you sleeping.
Yoghurt makes you healthy.
An apple a day keeps the doctor away.
A hot milky drink helps you go to sleep.
A cup of tea revives you.
Guinness is good for you.
Crusty bread makes your hair curl.
Brown eggs taste better than white ones.

Have you heard similar expressions? Do you agree or disagree with them?

"More die in the United States of too much food than too little."
J. K. Galbraith.

At different times in different countries there have been different ideas of beauty. The rich would always want to look fat in a society where food was scarce and to look thin in a society where food was plentiful. The current interest in slimming is because of fashion as well as health. However, overeating causes a variety of illnesses.

Do you know what they are? Are you overweight/average/underweight? Does it worry you? Have you ever been on a diet? What did you eat? What foods should you eat if you want to lose weight? What should you eat if you want to put on weight?

"One should eat to live, not live to eat."
Molière.

"When we consume a large steak we are eating something that may have used up enough grain to keep a family in the drought-stricken areas of Africa for a week."
Kenneth Mellanby, Can Britain Feed Itself?

"Year by year, while the world's population has increased, the food supply has increased more. (But)... supplies of nourishing food could be enormously increased if, in the richer countries of the world, people were prepared to eat some of the food they feed to their pigs and cattle... and to their pet dogs and cats."
Dr Magnus Pyke, Hunger and Humanity.

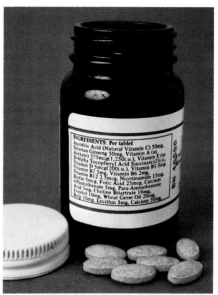

I WISH...

Mr Mannering J. C. Mannering.

Secretary Your call from New York's on line one, sir. Paris has just come through on line two and I've got a call from Tokyo on line four.

Mr Mannering Ask them to ring back tomorrow, Judy. Tell them ... tell them I'm not here. It's far too late. I wish I wasn't here. I've had enough today.

Secretary But sir, they're urgent, all of them.

Mr Mannering Do you know something, Judy? I wish I was at home now, in front of the television with a cup of cocoa!

Paula Look at that! It's pouring with rain again, and I've got to walk to the station.

Diane Typical British weather!

Paula It's all right for old Mannering. His Rolls-Royce is downstairs waiting to take him home.

Diane Mmm. I wish I had a chauffeur-driven Rolls.

Paula I wish I had a car, any car. I'm going to get soaked tonight!

Tony Hello, James. still here?

James Yes. I'm waiting to see Mr Mannering.

Tony You don't usually work in the evenings.

James I wish I wasn't working this evening. There's a good concert on.

Tony Oh well. Perhaps he'll call you soon.

James I hope he does!

Alan Haven't you finished yet?

Lorraine No. I wish I had. I can't go until I've completed this report.

Alan Can't you do it tomorrow?

Lorraine I wish I could, but Mannering wants it tonight.

Shirley Evening, Joan.

Joan Evening, Shirley. I don't feel like working tonight.

Shirley Neither do I. I hate this kind of work.

Joan Why do you do it then?

Shirley I wish I didn't have to! But we need the money. My husband's out of work again.

Joan I know what you mean. I wish I'd learnt to type, or something like that.

Shirley We can all wish! I left school at fourteen. I wish I hadn't, but there was no choice in those days. Youngsters have so many opportunities nowadays. I wish we'd had the chances. I'd never have ended up as a cleaner.

Joan Come on Shirley, let's have a cup of tea.

PC Look at that, Sergeant. There are still lights on in the insurance company again.

Sergeant Yes, it looks nice and warm, doesn't it? I sometimes wish I worked there.

PC Do you really?

Sergeant Mmm. Sometimes. A nice office, a desk, secretaries everywhere. It can't be bad.

PC And the boss's Rolls outside!

Sergeant Still, you know what they say: 'the grass is always greener on the other side of the hill.'

PC I suppose you're right, Sarge. Hey, that Rolls is on a double yellow line.

Sergeant Oh, yes. Give him a parking ticket. He can afford it!

Exercise 1

1 I wish I was on holiday.
I wish I was in Hawaii.
Where do you wish you were now?
Do you wish you were in bed?/at home?/on the beach?

2 I'm a student.
I wish I was an actor.
What do you wish you were?

Exercise 2

I haven't got a car. *I wish I had a car.*
Make five sentences.

Exercise 3

It's raining.
I wish it wasn't raining.
He's working.
He wishes he wasn't working.
Continue.
1 The phones are ringing.
2 It's snowing.
3 She's sitting in an office.
4 He's waiting.

Exercise 4

He hasn't finished yet.
He wishes he had finished.
I didn't learn to type.
I wish I had learnt to type!
Continue.
1 They haven't done their homework.
2 She left school at fourteen.
3 I haven't seen that film.
4 He lost his wallet.

Unit 42

THE HAPPIEST DAYS OF YOUR LIFE?

Some people say that your schooldays are the happiest days of your life. Here are six people talking about their schooldays.

Sally Jennings works in an advertising agency.

'I went to the local grammar school. It was an all-girls' school, and we all had to wear uniform. That uniform! I really hated it! We had to wear white socks, white blouses, matching blue skirts and blazers, and one of those ... you know ... funny little hats. Ooh! And we had to wear ties, really! We didn't mix much with children from other schools. It was a bit snobbish, I suppose. The syllabus was very academic. We never did things like cookery or needlework. I was glad at the time but I wish they'd taught us a few ... a few basics. I can't even make a decent omelette. I didn't like games, either – a lot of girls running round a hockey field on a freezing cold January afternoon. I hated it! Oh and another thing I regret ... I wish the school had been co-educational. I was terribly shy of boys for a couple of years after I left school ... simply because I hadn't met many.'

Freddie Tapper is a successful self-employed builder. He went to a secondary modern school.

'School? I left when I was 15, and I was glad to get out. I knew exactly what I wanted to do. I wanted to start earning a living as soon as possible ... in the real world. Most of the teachers were boring, and they didn't seem to understand us. They lived in a different world. They couldn't understand that we didn't want the things they wanted — you know, Shakespeare and all that rubbish! I'd have left earlier if I could. I think teachers are overpaid, and their holidays are too long. I don't know what they're always complaining about. I'm sorry I had to go to school at all!'

Samantha Wharton is the personnel manager of a department store.

'I was at a big comprehensive – nearly 2000 students. Because it was so big there was a wide choice of subjects and I liked that. I suppose it was a bit impersonal sometimes. I often wished it had been smaller, but the teaching was very good and there were lots of extra activities. I played in the school orchestra – not very well – and helped to produce the school newspaper. I think comprehensives could be improved. A lot of my friends left at 16, and they now regret leaving so early. Some of them would have done very well academically, if they had been encouraged enough. Still, maybe things are different now.'

William Bunter is a civil servant. He's a senior official in the Foreign Office.

'I went to Eton, actually. I suppose I had a very privileged education. Academic standards were very high and I was able to go on to Oxford. The thing I remember most is the comradeship. The friendships I made there have lasted through my life. Sports were very important for me – I believe that team games teach people to work together, and we played every afternoon. There's been a lot of bad publicity about corporal punishment in schools. I was often beaten but it didn't do me any harm. Maybe young people would be better behaved these days if there were more discipline in schools. My only regret about boarding-school is that I didn't get to know my parents very well. I didn't see much of them after the age of eight. I've thought a lot about the problems, but I'd like to send both of my sons to Eton. I've already reserved their places.'

Joyce Brown is a housewife.

'I was brought up in the country and I went to the little village school. We were all together – boys and girls of all ages. It was like one big, happy family. It was difficult for the teacher of course – different ages and abilities – but the older children helped the younger ones. I think it was a good preparation for life. I wish they'd never closed it. My children have to travel four miles by bus to the school in town. My schooldays were very happy. I never passed any exams, but I don't regret going to my little village school.'

Darren Andrews was at a comprehensive school. He's unemployed.

'I left last year when I was 18. I passed all my exams, but I still haven't been able to find a job. I wish I'd applied for university, but even with a degree, there's no guarantee of work nowadays. I wish I'd chosen different subjects. I specialized in English Literature, History, and Latin. I enjoyed doing them, but you see ... most of the jobs these days are on the technical side. I think schools ought to give more advice on careers and there should be more specific job preparation. If I'd known more about job possibilities, I'd've done other subjects.'

Some types of secondary school found in England.

Grammar school: State or independent secondary schools. They are selective and take more academically able children, up to the age of 16 or 18. There are state grammar schools in only a few areas now.

Secondary modern: State schools in areas which also have grammar schools. The pupils usually leave at 16, or transfer to a grammar school or college.

Comprehensive: Nowadays the normal secondary school in most areas. They take pupils of all abilities, and have replaced both grammar and secondary modern schools.

Public schools: Independent, private schools, taking pupils from 13–18 years. Most of the pupils are boarders. (They live in the school.) Eton is the most famous.

Exercise
What about your schooldays?
What do/did you like?
What don't/didn't you like?
What about uniforms? games? punishment? subjects? teachers? extra activities? travel?
Is/Was it co-educational or single-sex?
What changes would you make/would you have made?

Announcer This is the third and final stage of the 'Miss Britain' competition. We have seen all the contestants in bathing-costumes and in evening dresses, and the judges have selected our six finalists. The last stage is the interview, and in this stage our contestants will be judged on charm, intelligence and personality.

Listen to the interviews, and complete the chart at the bottom of the page.

Exercise
Ask and answer about each of the contestants:
Where's she from? How old is she? What does she do? What are her hobbies? What's her ambition? If she could have one wish, what would she wish for?

If you were a judge, which would you choose, and why? Listen to the results, and complete this chart:

Place	Name	Prize-money	Holiday
3rd			
2nd			
1st			

Beauty contests: points of view

'I never watch beauty contests. They're like a cattle market! I think they insult the intelligence of women. No woman with any self-respect would ever enter a competition like this. I find them totally degrading!'

'I certainly don't take them seriously. They're harmless fun, really. I mean, you see prettier girls every day in shops and offices. But people earn a living from their intelligence, or from their abilities. Why shouldn't they make money from their appearance?'

'I occasionally watch them, but I don't think I'd like them if I were a woman. After all, a lot of girls would look just as good with the make-up, clothes and lights. Anyway, beauty's only skin deep. I often feel irritated when I'm watching a beauty contest. The values are false.'

'I always watch them. I like looking at pretty girls. I'd rather watch a beauty contest than a programme about politics. There isn't enough glamour in the world. If you don't like it, you can always switch off the television!'

MISS BRITAIN

Contestant	Number	Age	Occupation	Hobbies	Ambition	Wish
MISS LANCASHIRE Grace Field	14	17	shop assistant	dressmaking cooking	to work with children	World peace
MISS DORSET Victoria Hardy						
MISS NORFOLK Lynn King						
MISS GWENT Myfanwy Lloyd						
MISS STRATHCLYDE Dawn Munro						
MISS WARWICKSHIRE Kerry Talbot						

OPERATION IMPOSSIBLE

Unit 45

M Now, 006. I want you to look at these pictures carefully. This could be the most important mission of your life. At last we've got the chance to break the biggest crime syndicate in the world – SMASH. Look at the man on the right. He's the one we've been after for years.

006 Who is he?

M We think he's the one that controls SMASH. He's certainly the one that ordered the murder of 003, the one that planned the hijacking of the jumbo jet full of world leaders, and he organizes the biggest drug-smuggling operation in the world.

006 Do we know his name?

M We know some of them. Otto Krugerand, that's the name he uses in legitimate business. Dr Nada, that's the name he was using in Vienna last year. John Smith, that's the signature he left in a hotel register in Bangkok.

006 Who's the gorilla standing behind him?

M Ah, Slojob. He's the bodyguard who travels everywhere with Krugerand, and the only person he trusts. He's an expert assassin. He's the one who fed 004 to the crocodiles.

006 How charming! What about the woman?

M Don't you recognize her?

006 No, I've never seen her before.

M You would have recognized her, if she hadn't had plastic surgery, and dyed her hair. Think back to Beirut.

006 Not Heidi Schwartz! She's the one who arranged the pipeline explosion, and then vanished into thin air!

M She's also Krugerand's wife, and the only pilot he allows to fly his private plane.

006 Who's the little guy wearing thick glasses?

M That's Professor Beratski, the mad scientist who defected from Moldania. He's an expert on laser technology, and the first man who's been able to perfect a space laser weapon. Krugerand is planning to build a private space-rocket which could put a satellite into orbit. Do you understand the importance of this, 006? If they got a laser weapon into space, they could hold the world to ransom. That's something which must not happen, 006!

M Take a look at this picture, 006.

006 It's an oil-rig.

M It looks like it, doesn't it? It belongs to Krugerand's oil company. It's a rig that's supposed to be drilling for oil in the Indian Ocean. Below it, there's a vast undersea complex.

006 The superstructure looks odd.

M In fact it conceals the launch-pad they're going to use for the rocket.

006 That must be a radar scanner, there.

M Yes. It's the scanner they'll use to track the rocket, but they can also see anything that tries to get near the rig. It's going to be very difficult to get you in, 006.

006 There's a helicopter pad.

M We think that would be too dangerous. Look at the helicopter closely. It carries air-to-air missiles which could destroy any aircraft approaching the rig.

006 How are we going to do it then?

M Go home and pack. We're flying you to Scotland tonight for two weeks of intensive mini-submarine training.

006 That sounds fun!

M And 006, try not to be late for the plane this time.

Exercise 1

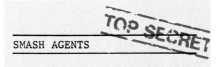

```
               TOP SECRET
SMASH AGENTS


KRUGERAND
controller of oil company/
millionaire/leader of SMASH

SLOJOB
killer of 004/expert assassin/
black belt karate

BERATSKI
defector from Moldania/laser
expert/inventor, space weapon

HEIDI
plastic surgery/pilot/married
Krugerand/met 006, Beirut
```

Krugerand's the | who controls an oil
one | that company.
He's the one | who 's a millionaire.
| that |

Make more sentences like this.

Exercise 2

```
DETAILS:OIL-RIG    TOP SECRET

SUPERSTRUCTURE
for hiding rocket

SCANNER
for tracking rocket

LAUNCH PAD
for launching rocket

PIPES
for rocket fuel

HELICOPTER
for transporting supplies/
people, defending rig

LIFT
for reaching undersea complex

PRIVATE ARMY
for defending rig
```

What's that? It's the radar scanner
which | they'll use for tracking
that | the rocket.

Make more sentences.

Exercise 3

She's the woman. He met her in Beirut.
She's the woman he met in Beirut.

Continue.
1 003 was the agent. Slojob killed him.
2 Krugerand's the leader. We've been trying to catch him.
3 Smith was the name. He used it in Bangkok.
4 Heidi's the woman. Krugerand married her.
5 Beratski's the scientist. SMASH recruited him.
6 They're the people. 006 must stop them.

OPERATION ACCOMPLISHED

Exercise 1

Look at the itinerary opposite.

He went to Scotland, where he learnt to handle a mini-sub.

He went to London, where he was given a transmitter.

He was given a transmitter, which was put into the heel of his shoe.

Make complete sentences, using 'where' and 'which' about 006's itinerary.

When 006 reached the rig he climbed up one of the towers. He was looking for someone whose uniform he could steal, but the rig seemed deserted. He went into an empty cabin. As he was looking for a change of clothes, the guard, whose cabin he was searching, came in. He was surprised to see 006 in his black frogman's suit and 006 had no difficulty in silencing him with one blow to the neck. Fortunately the guard was about the same size as 006, and the uniform fitted perfectly. There was a pass in the pocket. The pass operated the lift which went down to the undersea complex.

Exercise 2

Look at the diagram opposite.

This is where 006 left the mini-sub. Look at the diagram, and make ten more sentences like this.

006 woke up with his hands tied behind his back. His head was throbbing. He was not alone. In the room were Krugerand, Slojob, Heidi, and the guard whose clothes he was wearing. And a beautiful girl, whose hands were also tied, was lying beside him. 006 recognized her instantly. She was Pip Kingsley, an American agent he'd met in Washington. 006 looked at his watch. The explosive device he'd put on the rig was timed to explode in 45 minutes. Krugerand noticed that 006 was awake.

'Welcome, Commander Fleming. We've been expecting you,' he said smiling. 'Unfortunately we haven't got time to show you around. Blast-off is in forty minutes. Slojob will take you to feed the sharks ... they must be very hungry by now.'

'I'm delighted to meet you, Krugerand. I've been looking forward to it. Thank you for your invitation. I've always been interested in big fish. See you later.'

'I don't think so, Commander. This will be your last mission. Slojob! Take Commander Fleming and Miss Kingsley to the aquarium.'

Slojob escorted them to Krugerand's private apartment. One wall was made of thick glass and behind it 006 could see the dark shapes of the sharks, cruising around. Slojob pushed them up a spiral staircase to a platform above the shark tank.

'Ladies first,' 006 said politely.

'No, no. After you,' replied Miss Kingsley with a smile on her face.

'You wouldn't refuse us a last cigarette, would you, Slojob?' 006 asked.

'I don't smoke,' Slojob grinned. 'And you should give up smoking, it's bad for your health.'

'Now, come on, Slojob. There are some cigarettes and a lighter in my pocket.' 006 indicated his jacket pocket.

'OK. But don't try anything.' Slojob reached into 006's pocket and took out the cigarettes and lighter. He was careful to keep his gun trained on 006 all the time. He took a cigarette out of the packet and pushed it into 006's mouth. He pressed the lighter with his thumb. The sudden force of the flame took him by surprise. At that moment 006 kicked him in the stomach. He fell backwards and disappeared into the tank. Within

seconds all that remained of him was a red pool of blood on the surface.

The lighter had dropped to the floor and was still burning and 006 was able to burn through the ropes which held his hands. He quickly released Miss Kingsley. He glanced at his watch.

'We haven't got much time,' he said. 'Can you fly a helicopter?'

'I can fly anything if I have to,' she replied calmly.

'Good. Go and get the engines started and be ready to go. If I'm not there in exactly ten minutes, go without me.'

006 ran back to the control room and walked calmly in. 'Good evening, gentlemen,' he said. Krugerand turned, and he was moving his hand towards his pocket when a jet of flame from 006's lighter threw him back across the room. 006 pointed the lighter at Beratski and Heidi while he pulled every switch on the control panel until it exploded and burst into flames. 006 ran quickly to the lift but it was on fire. He had five minutes left and he started to climb the ladder in the lift shaft. He was halfway up when he felt a hand grabbing at his ankles. It was Krugerand! 006 gripped the ladder tightly, turned and kicked Krugerand hard in the face. He fell back, screaming, into the flames below. The helicopter was already in the air, hovering about a metre above the pad. 006 leapt onto a wheel, shouting 'Take it up! Take it up!' The helicopter soared into the sky. A few seconds later there was a massive explosion as the rig went up. 006 managed to climb into the helicopter cabin. He sat back, reached into his pocket and took out his cigarettes. He put one in his mouth, 'Oh blast!' he said. 'I seem to have forgotten my lighter. You haven't got a light, have you?'

Unit 46

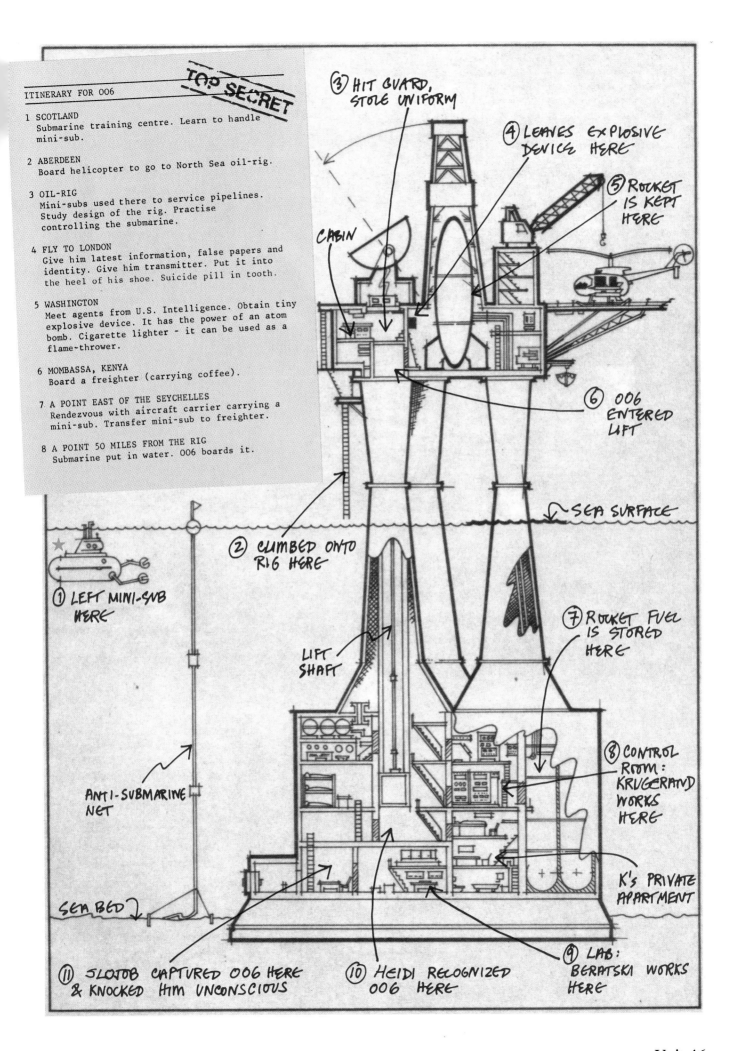

ITINERARY FOR 006

1 SCOTLAND
Submarine training centre. Learn to handle mini-sub.

2 ABERDEEN
Board helicopter to go to North Sea oil-rig.

3 OIL-RIG
Mini-subs used there to service pipelines. Study design of the rig. Practise controlling the submarine.

4 FLY TO LONDON
Give him latest information, false papers and identity. Give him transmitter. Put it into the heel of his shoe. Suicide pill in tooth.

5 WASHINGTON
Meet agents from U.S. Intelligence. Obtain tiny explosive device. It has the power of an atom bomb. Cigarette lighter - it can be used as a flame-thrower.

6 MOMBASSA, KENYA
Board a freighter (carrying coffee).

7 A POINT EAST OF THE SEYCHELLES
Rendezvous with aircraft carrier carrying a mini-sub. Transfer mini-sub to freighter.

8 A POINT 50 MILES FROM THE RIG
Submarine put in water. 006 boards it.

③ HIT GUARD, STOLE UNIFORM

④ LEAVES EXPLOSIVE DEVICE HERE

⑤ ROCKET IS KEPT HERE

CABIN

⑥ 006 ENTERED LIFT

SEA SURFACE

② CLIMBED ONTO RIG HERE

① LEFT MINI-SUB HERE

⑦ ROCKET FUEL IS STORED HERE

LIFT SHAFT

⑧ CONTROL ROOM: KRUGERAND WORKS HERE

ANTI-SUBMARINE NET

K's PRIVATE APARTMENT

SEABED

⑪ SLOJOB CAPTURED 006 HERE & KNOCKED HIM UNCONSCIOUS

⑩ HEIDI RECOGNIZED 006 HERE

⑨ LAB: BERATSKI WORKS HERE

Unit 46

Quiz master Our next contestant on 'Student Mastermind' is Victoria Bamber, who is a student at Sandpool Comprehensive. I'll just remind you of the rules, Miss Bamber. You have two minutes in which to answer as many questions as possible. If you do not know the answer, you should say, 'Pass'. I shall then go on to the next question. If you answer incorrectly, I shall then give the correct answer. You will get one point for each correct answer. If two contestants have the same number of points at the end, the one who has the fewest number of passes will be the winner. Are you ready?

Victoria Yes.

QM Can you name the President of the United States whose early career was in Hollywood?

Victoria Er ... Reagan. Ronald Reagan.

QM Correct. What is an instrument which shows the direction of north?

Victoria A compass?

QM Correct. Can you tell me the name of the sea where eels go to breed and die?

Victoria Er ... um ... pass.

QM Name the person who became the first woman prime minister of Britain?

Victoria Mary ... er, sorry ... Margaret Thatcher.

QM I'll accept that. What is the date when the United States celebrates its independence?

Victoria The fourth of July.

QM Correct. What do we call a person who always expects the best to happen?

Victoria Er ... an optimist.

QM Correct. Can you tell me the language which was spoken in the Roman Empire?

Victoria Italian?

QM No, wrong. The correct answer is Latin. What is the office people visit when they want advice about their marriage?

Victoria Pass.

QM Who was the Egyptian queen whose beauty was famous throughout the world?

Victoria Cleopatra.

QM That's correct. What's the newspaper column where jobs are advertised?

Victoria Er ... the job adverts?

QM Can you be more exact?

Victoria No. I can't think of it.

QM I'm afraid I can't give you that. We were looking for 'Situations Vacant'. Now can you tell me ...

STUDENT MASTERMIND

(DING) I've started, so I'll finish. Can you tell me the name of the French Emperor whose final battle was at Waterloo?

Victoria Napoleon Bonaparte.

QM Correct. And at the end of that round Victoria Bamber has scored seven points. You passed on two. The sea where eels go to breed and die is the Sargasso Sea, and the office people visit when they want advice about their marriage is the 'Marriage Guidance Council'. Thank you. Can we have our next contestant, please?

Exercise 1
Now practise the game with a partner.

Questions

1 What's a person who breaks into a house and steals things?
2 Who was the boxer whose most famous words were 'I am the greatest'?
3 What do we call a shop where bread is sold?
4 What is the day when Christians celebrate the birth of Jesus?
5 What's the place where you stand and wait for a train?
6 What's a tool which is used for digging?
7 Can you tell me the unusual public transport which is used in San Francisco?
8 Can you name the American president who was assassinated in 1963?
9 What do the British call the time of year when leaves fall from the trees?
10 Name the two young lovers whose tragic story was made into a play by Shakespeare.

Answers: ɹǝᴉɥnſ puɐ oǝɯoᴚ / uɯnʇnɐ / ʎpǝuuǝʞ ˙Ⅎ uɥoſ / ɹɐɔ-ǝlqɐɔ / ǝpɐds / s,ɹǝʞɐq / ʎɐᗡ sɐɯʇsᴉɹɥↃ / s,ɹǝʞɐq / ᴉl∀ pǝɯɯɐɥnW / ɹɐlƃɹnq

Exercise 2
Work with a partner. One of you uses List A, the other uses List B. Each of you writes down ten questions, using the words *who/which/where/when/whose* given in brackets in the list. Your question must give the answer provided in the list. For example:

Neil Armstrong (who)
Q *Can you tell me the name of the first man who walked on the moon?*
A *Neil Armstrong.*

widower (whose)
Q *What do you call a man whose wife has died?*
A *A widower.*

Now, with books closed, ask your partner the questions you have prepared. Your partner will then ask you to answer the questions he or she has prepared.

List A
Neil Armstrong (who)
sailor (who)
receipt (which)
submarine (which)
newsagent's (where)
casino (where)
golden wedding (when)
careers advisory service (when)
widow (whose)
Josephine Bonaparte (whose)

List B
widower (whose)
Columbus (who)
sleeping-pill (which)
driving licence (which)
left-luggage office (where)
butcher's (where)
job centre (when)
silver wedding (when)
Yoko Ono (whose)
pilot (who)

THE DAILY GAZETTE

Thursday May 27   No 8158   Price 30p

100 mph gales cause chaos

Strong winds, which at times reached speeds of 100 mph, brought havoc to many parts of Britain yesterday.

THE GALES, which were the worst in living memory, combined with high tides to cause devastation in some coastal regions. The government has sent troops to assist the emergency services in the North West, which has been hit particularly hard. Sea-walls, which have been broken in many places by unusually high tides, are being repaired urgently. Local authorities hope to contain the situation before the high tides, which are expected this evening. Calls have been issued for volunteers to help local council workmen, who have been working through the night. Many parts of Fleetwood, where the sea-wall collapsed entirely, are under two metres of water. Residents whose homes were flooded took refuge in the upstairs rooms. Men from the Fylde Naval Station, who have rescued hundreds of families, were visited by the Prime Minister during the evening.

● In Stoke-on-Trent, a woman, who was walking to work, was killed by a falling chimney.

● On the M6 Motorway, between Lancaster and Preston, a high-sided vehicle, which was carrying dangerous chemicals, was blown over. The north-bound carriageway was blocked for several hours.

● In Blackpool, hotels and shops which face the seafront are busy repairing windows which were blown in.

● Homes in Clitheroe, where electrical cables were blown down, were without electricity for eight hours.

● In Whitehaven, where fishing boats were torn from their moorings, the damage has been estimated at £200,000.

● A Spanish freighter, which was on its way to Liverpool, is missing in the Irish Sea. Air Sea Rescue helicopters are searching the area.

Mystery explosion in Indian Ocean

AN OIL-RIG in the Indian Ocean mysteriously exploded yesterday. The oil-rig, which had been drilling test wells, belonged to the Krugerand Corporation. A series of bright flashes, which were observed by ships 100 km away, preceded shock waves of unusual force. Several ships, which rushed to the rescue, have been searching for survivors but so far none have been found. It is not known how many people were working on the rig and the Krugerand Corporation, which is based in Switzerland, would not comment on the explosion.

Widow's defiance continues

MRS FLORENCE HAMILTON is still refusing to move from her old home. Tadworth local council, who have been trying to rehouse her for several months, have been unable to gain entry. The house, which the council wish to demolish to make way for redevelopment, now stands alone, surrounded by a mountain of rubble. Two council officials, who were trying to enter the house in the early hours of yesterday morning, were forced to retreat hastily when Mrs Hamilton turned her two pet alsatians loose. The dogs, Caesar and Nero, seem to be as determined as their owner, whose final words to the council were, 'I'm not b... moving, and that's that!' The council are reluctant to call in the police to remove Mrs Hamilton, whose plight has brought in many letters of support and encouragement from the general public.

Kidnap girl found

CAROLINE ROLAN, who police have been looking for since last Monday, has been found safe and well. Fourteen year old Caroline was found in a deserted house in Hackney after extensive police enquiries. A man and woman have been arrested and charged with the kidnapping.

'Wonderdrug' banned by DoH

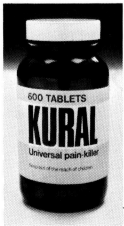

THE so-called wonderdrug 'Kural' which some doctors have been prescribing as a pain-killer, has been banned by the Department of Health. After extensive clinical trials over a number of years the drug has been found to produce alarming side-effects. 'Kural', which the manufacturers say produces almost miraculous results, is certainly very effective as a pain-killer. Unfortunately the drug seems to speed up the ageing process, which leads to premature hair loss, stiffening of the joints, loss of memory and, eventually, premature senile dementia.

Unit 48

FORMAL CORRESPONDENCE

139 Elm Tree Avenue
London SW13
15th August, 1982

Dear Sir,

I am writing to enquire about some items of laundry which were lost in your hotel laundry service. I was staying at the Haughty House Hotel from August 3rd until August 6th. On the morning of the 5th, I handed in my laundry bag and when it was returned the next day, I discovered that two socks were missing. One was brown, the other bright yellow. I also discovered that a shirt, which had also been laundered, had lost all its buttons. The housekeeper, to whom I complained, told me that the items would be posted on to me. I have heard nothing. I would also like to mention the question of compensation for the shirt, which was ruined. I bought it for £15 only a week previously.

Yours faithfully,
Barry Foot

---

139 Elm Tree Avenue
London SW13
22nd August, 1982

For the personal attention
of Sir Basil Haughty.

Dear Sir Basil,

I enclose a copy of a letter, which I sent to your hotel in Torquay. The manager, to whom I addressed it, replied in a most unsatisfactory way. I enclose his reply. I am most shocked that a hotel in which I have stayed on several occasions should reply in such an unhelpful fashion. I hope that you will take this matter up on my behalf.

Yours sincerely,
Barry Foot .

---

42 Winslow Avenue.
Guildford.
Surrey.
3rd March. 1982

Dear Sir,

Exactly one week ago, I purchased a polo-neck pullover from your Guildford store — the one in the High Street. I had worn the pullover only twice when I was amazed to discover a hole in the left sleeve. What is more, the pullover was not cheap. I believe in paying for quality. When I took the pullover back to the salesperson from whom I had bought it, she refused to exchange it and referred me to the manager. She too refused to exchange it. I am writing to you in the hope of gaining satisfaction. I have bought several pullovers from your store recently all of which have developed holes in the sleeves. I enclose the pullover and the receipt which shows the price and the date on which it was purchased.

Yours faithfully
Alfred King (Major retired)

Haughty House Hotel
Cliff Drive, Torquay, Devon

B. Foot Esq.
139 Elm Tree Ave.
London SW13

21st August 1982

Dear Mr. Foot,

Thank you for your letter in which you complained about our laundry service. May we remind you that the form on which you listed the items for laundering, states quite clearly that the hotel can accept no responsibility for lost items of clothing. The bag in which you placed your clothes, has the same warning clearly printed on it. We apologise for the inconvenience and hope that we shall have the pleasure of your custom on future occasions.

Yours sincerely,

Simon Lazenby

Manager

Haughty House Hotels Group
Head Office: Torres St., London W1.

1st September 1982

Dear Mr. Foot,

Thank you for your letter of August 22nd to Sir Basil Haughty, for whom I am replying. Sir Basil is unable to answer personal correspondence about hotels in the group. All correspondence should be addressed to the manager of the hotel concerned, to whom I have passed your letter.

Yours sincerely,

Anna Scales

Private Secretary to Sir Basil Haughty

Sparks & Fraser Ltd.
HEAD OFFICE   Butcher Street, London W2

Major A. King
42 Winslow Avenue
Guildford

12th April 1982

Dear Major King,

Please find enclosed the pullover about which you complained in your letter of March 3rd. We regret that we cannot exchange it. Our Guildford Manager, to whom you first complained, was perfectly correct in refusing to do so. She was carrying out company policy, which states that goods which have been worn cannot be exchanged. Our quality control department investigated your complaint and came to the conclusion that the sleeve in which the hole appeared, must have been subjected to unusual stress. Perhaps in your work or your leisure you constantly rub your elbows on a rough surface. Perhaps leather patches sewn onto the elbows would extend its life. The leather patches, to which I refer, are on sale at our Guildford branch, the one from which you bought the pullover. I am sure the staff there will be only too ready to help.

Yours sincerely,

Harriet Littlewood (Mrs.)

WHO, WHICH, THAT, WHOSE, WHOM

Exercise 1
He's the man. He saw Mary.
He's the man | *who* | *saw Mary.*
          | *that* |

That's the car. It crashed.
That's the car | *which* | *crashed.*
         | *that* |

1 She's the swimmer. She's just won the gold medal.
2 They're the keys. They open the drawers.
3 That's the travel agency. It sells cheap tickets.
4 Those are the astronauts. They were in orbit for six months.

Exercise 2
He's the man. Mary saw him.
He's the man Mary saw. or
He's the man | *who* | *Mary saw.*
          | *that* |

That's the car. He bought it yesterday.
That's the car he bought yesterday. or
That's the car | *which* | *he*
         | *that* |

bought yesterday.

1 These are the books. I use them in class.
2 They're the spies. The police have been watching them.
3 He's the criminal. The police are looking for him.
4 That's the name. I couldn't remember it yesterday.

Exercise 3
Mr Cox is the manager. He saw Ann.
Mr Cox, who saw Ann, is the manager.

The blue car crashed. It was a Ford.
The blue car, which was a Ford, crashed.

1 Those men saved my life. They pulled me from the burning car.
2 That woman travels everywhere by private plane. She's a millionairess.
3 That hotel's near the beach. It's the most expensive.
4 Those birds migrate to Antarctica. They breed near the North Pole.

Exercise 4
Ann has got the job. Mr Cox saw her.
Ann, who Mr Cox saw, has got the job.

The car crashed. He had only bought it the day before.
The car, which he had only bought the day before, crashed.

1 My parents send their best wishes. You met them last month.
2 The parcel contained a bomb. They had opened it carefully.
3 The match will be shown on TV tonight. They filmed it this afternoon.
4 His sisters are identical twins. I saw them last year.

Exercise 5
The book is about Dennis Thatcher. His wife became Prime Minister.
The book is about Dennis Thatcher whose wife became Prime Minister.

1 The film is about two people. Their plane crashed in the jungle.
2 The play is about a king. His ambition was to rule the world.
3 The ballet is about a princess. Her step-mother hated her.
4 The song is about two young lovers. Their romance ended happily.

Exercise 6
My neighbour gave me some theatre tickets. Her brother is an actor.
My neighbour, whose brother is an actor, gave me some theatre tickets.

A man from our village was on TV last night. I teach his children.
A man from our village, whose children I teach, was on TV last night.

1 Charlie Chaplin died in 1977. His films amused millions.
2 Rod Lee, the actor, has just won an Oscar. I know his sister.
3 Our teacher speaks English perfectly. Her parents are Greek.
4 The Taylor family now live in America. We bought their house.

Exercise 7
She's the woman. I wrote to her.
She's the woman to whom I wrote. (Very formal.)
She is the woman who I wrote to.

That's the hotel. I stayed in it.
That is the hotel in which I stayed. (Very formal.)
That's the hotel which I stayed in.

Transform these sentences, first in a formal style, then in an informal style.
1 They are the people. I was talking about them.
2 That is the dog. I was afraid of it.
3 Mr Cox is the manager. I am telephoning for him.
4 That is the tunnel. He went through it.
5 She is the lady. He argued with her.
6 She is the policewoman. The driver spoke to her.
7 That is the mistake. I am complaining about it.
8 He is the man. The novel was written by him.
9 There is the shop. I bought my radio from it.

Look at this.

The Pickwick School of English, London
Class: 7 (intermediate)   Date: 1st July

Name	From	Mother tongue	Age	Arrival date	Leaving date
Hans Schmidt	Zurich, Switzerland	German	18	30/6	29/7
Maria Perez	Monterrey, Mexico	Spanish	17	31/5	30/8
Paola Rossi	Turin, Italy	Italian	16	15/6	15/8
Rodrigo Cabral	São Paulo, Brazil	Portuguese	20	30/6	31/9

Exercise 8
1 *Hans is the one who comes from Zurich.*
2 *He's the one who speaks German.*
3 *He's the one who's leaving on July 29th.*
4 *Hans, who's from Zurich, speaks German.*
5 *Hans, who speaks German, is Swiss.*
6 *Hans, who's Swiss, is 18.*
7 *Hans, who's 18, arrived on June 30th.*
8 *Hans, who arrived on June 30th, is leaving on July 29th.*
9 *Hans, whose mother tongue is German, comes from Zurich.*
10 *Zurich, which is in Switzerland, is Hans' home town.*
Make sentences about all the students.

DESCRIBING THINGS

Lost property

A British Rail Lost Property, Waterloo.
B Oh, good morning. I left my brief-case on the train this morning. I wondered if it had been handed in.
A Which train, sir?
B Sorry, the 7.47 from Bourne-mouth.
A Can you describe the briefcase, sir?
B Er . . . yes. It's sort of a . . . well, an average-sized, rectangular, black leather briefcase with brass locks.
A We've got rather a lot like that, sir. Did it have your name on it?
B No, not my name. But it's got the initials 'J.R.' near the handle.
A Hang on, then, sir. I'll just go and have a look.

Exercise 1
Imagine you have lost something. Describe it to your partner without telling him what it is. Your partner has to guess.

Stolen car

A Metropolitan Police.
B My car's been stolen! It's gone!
A Calm down, sir. Could I have your name and address?
B Yes, Richard Lockwood, 3 Park Terrace, W.C.13.
A May I have a description of the vehicle, sir?
B It's a 1982 Escort, a silver-blue, four-door 1300GL model. Oh, and it's got a dark blue stripe along the sides, and a dent in the nearside front wing.
A But what's the registration, sir?
B PSV 439Y.
A I've got good news for you, sir. It hasn't been stolen. It's been towed away. It was parked on a double yellow line. You can collect it from the Police Compound, and you'd better bring your cheque-book with you!

Exercise 2
Describe somebody's car. Describe a car you would like to own.

The estate agent

A Rebecca Trueman speaking.
B Ah, Mrs Trueman. This is Fox and Connor, the estate agents. I think we've found a house that you may be interested in.
A Could you tell me something about it?
B It's in Redhill, near the station, as you requested. It's a rather attrac-tive four-bedroomed 1930s red-brick property. It's in very good decorative order, with a fitted kitchen.
A And the garden?
B There's a large, mature garden. Would you like to view it?
A Yes, I think it's worth a look. Could you put the details in the post?

Exercise 3
Describe somebody's house. Describe a house you would like to live in.

Exercise 4
Describe these rooms. Describe your ideal room. Describe the furniture you would put in it, and where you would put it. Describe a café or a restaurant that you have visited. De-scribe a room or office in the school.

Exercise 5
Try and describe an object to a part-ner using the diagram below. Your partner guesses what it is.

Note: This diagram shows the usual order of Adjectives. You won't often find them all in one sentence.

How much/ many?	What's it like?	How big?	What shape?	How old?	What colour?		What's the pattern?	Where's it from?	What's it made of?	What is it?
a/an	beautiful	little	square	old	pale	red	check	French	silk	scarf
one	nice	small	round	new	light	yellow	striped	English	cotton	blouse
three	ugly	medium-sized	oval	modern	bright	green	plain	Japanese	wooden	desk
some	clean	average-sized	rectangular	antique	dark	blue	flowered	German	leather	car
a few	dirty	large	pointed	19th century		brown	spotted	Italian	gold	house
several	cheap	big	triangular	1930s		black		Roman	metal	box
a lot of	expensive	long	flat	1982		white		Parisian	paper	

DESCRIBING PEOPLE

Listen to these people talking about their friends. Look at the example. Complete the other columns.

Name	Donna	Colin	Janet	Robert
Age	late teens			
Build	good figure			
Height	fairly tall			
Hair colour	black			
Hairstyle	long, wavy			
Face	heart-shaped, turned-up nose, full lips			
Eyes	blue, long eyelashes			
Complexion	olive-skinned			
Distinguishing features	dimples			
Dress				
Personality	lively, talkative			

Look at this

Age	Build	Height	Hair colour	Hairstyle	Face	Distinguishing features	Personality
young	fat	1.70 m	black	long	thin	beard (M)	quiet
middle-aged	thin	medium height	brown	short	long	moustache (M)	reserved
elderly	slim	average height	red	straight	round	side-burns (M)	thoughtful
old	plump	below average	fair	wavy	oval	unshaven (M)	calm
in his/her 30's	medium-build	tall	blonde	curly	square	clean-shaven (M)	moody
in his/her late teens	well-built (M)	short	grey	neat	heart-shaped (F)	a scar	unsociable
in his/her mid-20's	broad-shouldered (M)	tallish	white	untidy	high cheekbones	a beauty-spot (F)	sociable
in his/her early 40's	overweight	shortish	dyed	with plaits (F)	high forehead	a mole	sophisticated
			a brunette (F)	a fringe	thin lips	with freckles	lively
			a blonde (F)	swept back	full lips	with dimples	cheerful
				in a bun (F)	long nose	with spots	amusing
			a redhead (F)	pony-tail (F)	straight nose	with wrinkles	polite
				bald (M)	turned-up nose	with lines	reliable
			mousey	balding (M)	broken nose	with glasses	talkative
			dark	thinning (M)	a cleft chin	(well) made-up (F)	aggressive
				receding (M)	a pointed chin		friendly
					double chin		shy

Eyes	Complexion	Dress
blue	pale	smart
grey	sunburned/tanned	scruffy
brown	olive-skinned	well-dressed
long eyelashes	fair-skinned	casual
thick eyelashes	Oriental	conservative
bushy eyelashes	brown	elegant
thin eyebrows	black	fashionable

Describe these people. Describe yourself, another student, a famous person.

Unit 52

BUDGET DAY

The British government normally announces changes in taxation once a year. This usually happens in March when the Chancellor of the Exchequer reads his budget proposals in the House of Commons. He outlines the changes in taxation which will balance government income and expenditure for the next year. Sometimes the changes in indirect taxation take effect immediately. Many people try to 'beat the budget' by guessing which articles will increase in price, and buying them before the Chancellor makes his announcement.

The day before the budget

Julie Hello, darling. You're late.

Graham Yes. I went to the garage to get some petrol.

Julie But that only takes five minutes, doesn't it?

Graham Not today. There was a queue halfway down the road.

Julie Really? Why? There isn't another oil crisis, is there?

Graham No, no. They were all filling their tanks to beat the budget. Everybody expects a big increase in tax on petrol. I bought ten gallons!

Exercise 1

garage
He went to the garage to get some petrol.
Make sentences with:
1 bank
2 chemist's
3 library
4 newsagent's
5 butcher's
6 baker's
7 greengrocer's
8 florist's
9 tobacconist's
10 off-licence

Budget morning

Graham It says in the paper that they might increase taxes on electrical goods.

Julie Perhaps we should buy that new fridge/freezer we were looking at. What do you think?

Graham Yes, we need one anyway.

Julie Can you get to the shop at lunchtime?

Graham I'm afraid not. Look, we know how much it is. Why don't you write a cheque, and send Stuart to buy it?

Julie All right. If you're sure we can afford it.

Graham It was an Electrolux 1241, wasn't it? Send him to get it at the show-room in Highfield Road. They had it on special offer.

Exercise 2

He/her/post office/stamps.
He sent her to the post office to get some stamps.
Continue.
1 They/him/newsagent's/a map.
2 She/them/off-licence/wine.
3 My boss/me/stationer's/paper.
4 We/John/supermarket/fruit.

4.30, Budget afternoon

Julie Stuart, switch on the television, will you? I want to hear the news about the budget.

Stuart Right, Mum.

Newsreader And here are the major points about today's budget again. In order to raise £60 million, the government proposes to increase the duty on tobacco. This will mean an increase of 15p on a packet of cigarettes, which should please anti-smoking campaigners. The Chancellor has also increased the duty on beer, wines, and spirits in order to raise an extra £400 million in revenue. The government has also increased petrol tax by 15% so as to encourage energy saving. Value Added Tax has been reduced by 2% so as to stimulate the economy. This will mean that household goods – televisions, washing-machines, fridges, etc., will go down in price.

Exercise 3

In order to raise £60 million, they increased tobacco duty.
So as to raise £60 million, they increased tobacco duty.
They increased tobacco duty in order to raise £60 million.
They increased tobacco duty so as to raise £60 million.
Make sentences in each of these four ways about each proposal in the table below.

Proposal	Purpose
Increase tobacco duty.	Raise £60 million.
Put up the duty on wines, beers and spirits.	Raise £400 million.
Increase petrol tax by 15%.	Encourage energy saving.
Reduce VAT by 2%.	Stimulate the economy.
Reduce income-tax.	Increase incentives.
Subsidize heavy fuel.	Help industry.
Impose import controls.	Protect home industries.
Sell parts of the steel industry.	Raise £1,000 million.
Give financial help for home insulation.	Encourage energy saving.
Increase old age pensions.	Protect old people from inflation.

DO IT YOURSELF

Do It Yourself magazine organizes a competition every summer to find the 'Handyman of the Year'. The winner this year is Mr Roy Miller, a Sheffield postman. A journalist and a photographer have come to his house. The journalist is interviewing Mr Miller for an article in the magazine.

Journalist Well, I'm very impressed by all the work you've done on your house, Mr Miller. How long have you been working on it?

Mr Miller I first became interested in do-it-yourself several years ago. You see, my son Paul is disabled. He's in a wheel-chair and I just had to make alterations to the house. I coudn't afford to pay workmen to do it. I had to learn to do it myself.

Journalist Had you had any experience of this kind of work? Did you have any practical skills?

Mr M No. I got a few books from the library but they didn't help very much. Then I decided to go to evening classes so that I could learn basic carpentry and electrics.

Journalist What sort of changes did you make to the house?

Mr M First of all, practical things to help Paul. You never really realize the problems handicapped people have until it affects your own family. Most government buildings, for example, have steps up to the door. They don't plan buildings so that disabled people can get in and out. We used to live in a flat, and of course, it was totally unsuitable. Just imagine the problems a disabled person would have in your house. We needed a large house with wide corridors so that Paul could get from one room to another. We didn't have much money and we had to buy this one. It's over ninety years old and it was in a very bad state of repair.

Journalist Where did you begin?

Mr M The electrics. I completely re-wired the house so that Paul could reach all the switches. I had to lower the light switches and raise the power-points. I went on to do the whole house so that Paul could reach things and go where he wanted.

Journalist What else did you do?

Mr M By the time I'd altered everything for Paul, do-it-yourself had become a hobby. I really enjoyed doing things with my hands. Look, I even installed smoke-alarms.

Journalist What was the purpose of that?

Mr M I was very worried about fire. You see, Paul can't move very quickly. I fitted them so that we would have plenty of warning if there were a fire. I put in a complete burglar-alarm system. It took weeks. The front door opens automatically, and I'm going to put a device on Paul's wheelchair so that he'll be able to open and close it when he wants.

Journalist What are you working on now?

Mr M I've just finished the kitchen. I've designed it so that he can reach everything. Now I'm building an extension so that Paul will have a large room on the ground floor where he can work.

Journalist There's a £10,000 prize. How are you going to spend it?

Mr M I'm hoping to start my own business so that I can convert ordinary houses for disabled people. I think I've become an expert on the subject.

Look at this

| I did this so that | he | could / couldn't | do that. |
| | this | would / wouldn't | happen. |

| I'm doing this / I do this | so that | he | can / can't | do that. |
| | | this | will / won't | happen. |

or

| So that | he | could / couldn't | do that, | I did this. |
| | this | would / wouldn't | happen, | |

| So that | he | can / can't | do that, | I'm doing this. / I do this. |
| | this | will / won't | happen, | |

Exercise 1

These are some of the things that Mr Miller did. Look at the chart, ask questions with *Why?/What's the purpose of ... ?'* and answer them.

Improvement	Purpose
swing gate, swing doors	Paul wouldn't have to use the handles.
level the path	The wheel-chair would move easily.
widen the doors	The wheel-chair could get through.
phones in every room	Paul could always get to one.
special bathroom	Paul could use it.
lower the light switches	Paul could reach them.
remove the steps, put in ramps	The wheel-chair could get in and out.

Exercise 2

Here are some of the things Mr Miller is going to do. Ask questions and answer them.

Plan	Purpose
a device on his wheelchair	He'll be able to open and close the front door.
install a lift	He'll be able to get upstairs on his own.
build an extension	He'll have a room on the ground floor.
convert mini-bus with a ramp	He'll be able to get in and out.
design a 'bleeper'	He can call me at any time.
build a workshop in the garden	I'll have somewhere to work.

TAKE CARE!

Look at this

Do this	so as in order	not to do that.	
Do this	to so as to in order to	avoid	that. doing that.
Do this	to prevent	that. something (from) happening. somebody (from) doing that.	

Exercise 1
Look at the expressions in Mandangani. Practise with a partner using:
How do you say (this) in Mandangani?
Can you translate (this) into Mandangani?
What does (that) mean in English?

Exercise 2
Why should we keep plastic bags away from babies?
To avoid the danger of suffocation.
or
To prevent babies from suffocating themselves.
Look at the table above. Ask questions about the warnings, and answer them.

MACDONALD
CONSTRUCTION (UK) LTD.
River Danga Irrigation Scheme
Advice to employees travelling to Mandanga for the first time.

CONFIDENTIAL

MEDICAL PRECAUTIONS
1 To avoid the possibility of infection, inoculations against typhoid, cholera, and yellow fever should be given before departure.
2 Mandanga is a malarial area. To prevent malaria, a course of anti-malaria tablets should be started two weeks before departure. In the evenings long-sleeved clothes should be worn to prevent mosquito bites.
3 When in camp always use a net in order to prevent mosquitos biting while you are asleep.
4 A thorough medical examination and a full dental checkup is advised before leaving the UK.
5 A spare pair of glasses is recommended.
6 Mandanga is a tropical country and certain precautions should be taken when working:
a To prevent heat exhaustion, take care to drink adequate quantities of fluid.
b Salt tablets may be taken to avoid dehydration.
c To prevent sunstroke, great care must be taken when working in direct sunlight.
d Sensible, loose-fitting lightweight clothes are recommended. Cotton is the best material.

HYGIENE
1 To avoid infection, water should be boiled or purified with tablets.
2 Fruit and vegetables should be washed thoroughly.

LOCAL CUSTOMS
1 Women should wear hats and long dresses when entering religious buildings. They should particularly avoid wearing trousers, shorts, or mini-skirts.
2 Shoes should be removed when entering private homes, to avoid giving offence to the householder.
3 So as not to cause offence, washing should never be hung out in public view. This particularly applies to underclothes.
4 Women should avoid wearing bikinis on public beaches.
5 In order not to seem rude, we would strongly advise learning a few expressions in Mandangani before arrival.
Here are a few essential expressions:

Whot ho	*Hello*
Tu dalu	*Goodbye*
Yup	*Yes*
Nok	*No*
Ta aw flee	*Thank you*
Ifi	*Please*
Ay up	*Excuse me*
Oop Zee	*Sorry*

SAFETY FIRST
To avoid danger of suffocation keep this plastic bag away from babies and young children.

Supertrack hi-fi stylus ST800E
Check your stylus regularly to avoid damaging your valuable records. Change it at the first sign of wear.

TEFL
Non-stick frying pan
To avoid scratching this pan, always use a wooden or plastic spatula. Avoid using metal implements at all times.

National Midland
Cheque Card
To prevent the possibility of someone misusing this cheque guarantee card, never keep it in the same place as your cheque-book.

Rollalong tyres
To prevent undue wear always check that the tyres are at the correct pressure. Stones should be removed from the tread to prevent them from damaging the tyre. At regular intervals change tyres to different wheels to avoid uneven wear.

Set of six Irish coffee glasses
Always place a spoon in the glass before pouring hot coffee into it. This will prevent the glass cracking.

Swanham's multigrade oil 20/50
To prevent undue engine wear always change the oil at regular intervals.

Bunter and Farmer
BISCUITS
In order to keep these biscuits in good condition store in a cool, dry place.

Announcer On 'TV Magazine' to-night we're looking at people who have given up regular jobs and high salaries to start a new way of life. First of all, we have two interviews with people who decided to leave the 'rat race'. Nicola Burgess spoke to them.

Nicola This is the Isle of Skye. Behind me you can see the croft belonging to Daniel and Michelle Burns, who gave up their jobs to come to this remote area of Scotland. Daniel was the sales manager of Hi-Vita, the breakfast cereal company, and Michelle was a successful advertising executive. Michelle, can you tell us what made you give up everything to come here?

Michelle Everything? That's a matter of opinion. A big house and two cars isn't everything! Dan and I both used to work long hours. We had to leave so early in the morning and we came home so late at night, that we hardly ever saw each other. We should have come here years ago, but we were earning such big salaries that we were afraid to leave our jobs. In the end we had so little time together that our marriage was breaking up. So two years ago, we took a week's holiday in the Scottish Highlands. We saw this place and we both fell in love with it. It was for sale, and we liked it so much that we decided to give up our jobs, and here we are!

Nicola How do you earn a living? If you don't mind me asking.

Michelle We don't need very much. We keep sheep and goats, grow our own vegetables. We've got a few chickens. It's a very simple life, and we're not in it for profit. We're still so busy that we work from five in the morning until eight at night, but we're together. We're happier than we've ever been and we're leading a natural life.

Nicola There must be some things you miss, surely.

Michelle I don't know. We knew such a lot of people in London, but they weren't real friends. We see our neighbours occasionally and there's such a lot to do on the farm that we don't have time to feel lonely. At least we see each other now.

A NEW WAY OF LIFE

Nicola The motor-bike I'm sitting on is a very special one. Special because it's been all the way round the world. It belongs to Luke Saunders, who has just returned to England after a three-year motor-cycle journey. Luke, what led you to leave your job and make this trip?

Luke I worked in a car factory on the assembly line. All I had to do was put four nuts on the bolts that hold the wheels on. It's done by robots now, and a good thing too! The job was so routine that I didn't have to think at all. I bought this Triumph 750 cc bike second-hand, fitted two panniers on the back and just set off for Australia.

Nicola What did you do for money?

Luke I had a bit of money to start with, but of course it didn't last long and I had to find work where I could. I've done so many different things – picked fruit, washed up, worked as a mechanic.

Nicola How did people react to you? In India, for example.

Luke Everywhere I went, the people were so friendly that problems seemed to solve themselves. There was such a lot of interest in the bike that it was easy to start a conversation. You know, often you can communicate without really knowing the language.

Nicola Did you ever feel like giving up, turning round and coming home?

Luke Only once, in Bangladesh. I became so ill with food poisoning that I had to go to hospital. But it didn't last long.

Nicola You've had such an exciting time that you'll find it difficult to settle down, won't you?

Luke I'm not going to. Next week I'm off again, but this time I'm going in the opposite direction! See you in about three years' time!

Exercise 1

The people were very friendly. He felt welcome.
The people were so friendly that he felt welcome.
Continue.
1 He was very old. He couldn't walk.
2 She was very busy. She didn't stop for lunch.
3 He was very late. He missed the train.
4 She's was very ill. She couldn't go out.
5 He had spent too much money. He couldn't buy a ticket.
6 There were too many people on the boat. It sank.

Exercise 2

The house was so beautiful that they bought it.
It was such a beautiful house that they bought it.
Continue.
1 The book was so interesting that she couldn't stop reading it.
2 The problems are so difficult that nobody can solve them.
3 The man was so friendly that everybody liked him.
4 The dog was so savage that the postman refused to deliver the letters.
5 The box was so heavy that she couldn't lift it.
6 The trip was so exciting that he's going again.

Exercise 3

He was such a good boxer that nobody ever beat him.
The boxer was so good that nobody ever beat him.
Continue.
1 It was such a dangerous job that nobody would do it.
2 She was such a good dancer that she won the prize.
3 They were such boring films that nobody watched them.
4 It was such a crazy story that nobody believed it.

LAST OF THE AIRSHIPS?

At 7.20 pm on May 6th 1937, the world's largest airship, the Hindenburg, floated majestically over Lakehurst airport, New Jersey, after an uneventful crossing from Frankfurt, Germany. There were 97 people on board for the first Atlantic crossing of the season. There were a number of journalists waiting to greet it. Suddenly radio listeners heard the commentator screaming 'Oh, my God! It's broken into flames. It's flashing … flashing. It's flashing terribly.' 32 seconds later the airship had disintegrated and 35 people were dead. The Age of the Airship was over.

The Hindenburg was the last in a series of airships which had been developed over 40 years in both Europe and the United States. They were designed to carry passengers and cargo over long distances. The Hindenburg could carry 50 passengers accommodated in 25 luxury cabins with all the amenities of a first class hotel. All the cabins had hot and cold water and electric heating. There was a dining-room, a bar and a lounge with a dance floor and a baby grand piano. The Hindenburg had been built to compete with the great luxury transatlantic liners. It was 245 metres long with a diameter of 41 metres. It could cruise at a speed of 125 km/h, and was able to cross the Atlantic in less than half the time of a liner. By 1937

it had carried 1000 passengers safely and had even transported circus animals and cars. Its sister ship, the Graf Zeppelin, had flown one and a half million kilometres and it had carried 13,100 passengers without incident.

The Hindenburg was filled with hydrogen, which is a highly flammable gas, and every safety precaution had been taken to prevent accidents. It had a smoking room which was pressurized in order to prevent gas from ever entering it. The cigarette lighters were chained to the tables and both passengers and crew were searched for matches before entering the ship. Special materials, which were used in the construction of the airship, had been chosen to minimize the possibility of accidental sparks, which might cause an explosion.

Nobody knows the exact cause of the Hindenburg disaster. Sabotage has been suggested, but experts at the time believed that it was caused by leaking gas which was ignited by static electricity. It had been waiting to land for three hours because of heavy thunderstorms. The explosion happened just as the first mooring rope, which was wet, touched the ground. Observers saw the first flames appear near the tail, and they began to spread quickly along the hull. There were a

number of flashes as the hydrogen-filled compartments exploded. The airship sank to the ground. The most surprising thing is that 62 people managed to escape. The fatalities were highest among the crew, many of whom were working deep inside the airship. After the Hindenburg disaster, all airships were grounded and, until recently, they have never been seriously considered as a commercial proposition.

Airships – achievements and disasters.

1852 1st airship (43.8 m long) flew over Paris.

1910 Five Zeppelin airships operated
– 14 commercial flights within Germany, carrying 35,000 people without injury.

1914 Military Zeppelins took part in
– 18 53 bombing raids on London, during First World War.

1919 British 'R34'. First transatlantic crossing. Both directions (10,187 km in 183 hours).

1921 British 'R38' broke up over Yorkshire, killing 15 passengers, 29 crew.

1925 US 'Shenandoah' (first helium airship) destroyed in a storm over Ohio. Heavy loss of life.

1926 Italian airship, the 'Norge', flew over North Pole.

1929 German Graf Zeppelin flew round the world. Began commercial transatlantic flights.

1930 British 'R101' (236 m long) crashed over Beauvais, France. Killed 48 out of 54 on board. British airship programme cancelled.

1931 US 'Akron' in service in USA – could carry 207 passengers.

1933 'Akron' wrecked in a storm.

1935 Sister ship, US 'Macon' wrecked.

1936 Hindenburg built. Carried 117 passengers in one flight.

1937 It crashed.

1938 'Graf Zeppelin II' completed. It never entered service.

1940 Both Graf Zeppelins scrapped.

1958 US Navy built a radar airship, the 'ZPG3–W'. (123 m long, 21 crew.)

1960 June. 'ZPG3–W' crashed in the sea.

1961 US Navy airship programme ended.

1975 US Goodyear company operating small airship fleet. The 'Europa' (58 m long) carries a pilot and six passengers.

EATING OUT

Eating Out
by Clement Harding

The Old Mill, The Quay,
Wardleton, Sussex
Open: Tuesday – Sunday
7–11.30 p.m.

This week we decided to look at a small family-run restaurant in the village of Wardleton. 'The Old Mill' is newly opened and overlooks the River Wardle, and we had heard several favourable comments about it. Because we had been advised to book early, we managed to get a nice table with a view of the quay. We were made very welcome and the service was excellent because it is a small family business. The proprietor, Jeff Dean, runs the kitchen himself and his wife, Nelly, showed us to our table.

Although the choice of items on the menu was very extensive, it was rather traditional. A long menu always worries me, because a large menu often means a large freezer! We started with Wardle Trout and although it was fresh, it was spoilt by the number of herbs. For my main course I chose the pepper steak, which was the speciality of the day. I thought

it was almost perfect because the chef had chosen excellent meat and it was cooked just long enough.

My wife ordered the roast lamb, and although the quality of the meat was good, she thought it was a little under-done. Though the vegetables were fresh, they came in very small portions and were rather over-cooked for our taste. However, the bread was fresh because it had been baked on the premises. I have often complained in this column about the difficulty of finding any restaurant which serves a fresh fruit salad. Luckily, this one did. Even though it must have been very time-consuming to prepare, it was a delight to see, and I had a second helping.

As usual I chose house wine, as this is often the best way to judge a restaurant's wine list. It was a French-bottled table wine which was quite satisfactory and reasonably priced. The bill, including coffee and brandy, came to £37, which was acceptable for the class of restaurant, although that did not include service.

Fast Food
by Rebecca Mitchell

Nashville Superburger Bar,
Leicester Square,
London
Open: 7 days a week, 24 hours a day

A new American fast-food chain has just opened its first restaurant in Britain. 'The Nashville Superburger Bar' is just off Leicester Square. Because of the success of McDonald's and Kentucky Fried Chicken, I was interested to see if Nashville had anything new to offer. The restaurant was so brightly-lit that I wished I'd brought my sunglasses. Once I'd got used to the light, I rather liked the green and orange plastic décor, which was very futuristic. The place was spotlessly clean – almost antiseptic! Although there was a long queue, service was incredibly fast. The menu was limited to a variety of hamburgers and prices were very reasonable. I had the 'Giant Superburger' which was served with a

generous helping of french fries. Although the burger itself was rather tasteless, there was a large selection of relishes on every table and the french fries were the best I've ever tasted. This kind of establishment obviously caters for young people in a hurry. I was amazed to see that many of the customers preferred to eat standing up even though there were seats available. Most of the customers were under 25 and alone. Everybody seemed to be drinking milk-shakes and although I'm not very fond of them I felt I should have one. Not much can go wrong with a milk-shake and it tasted as good or as bad as any other. Although it's a quick and efficient way of taking nourishment, you wouldn't choose 'The Nashville' for a quiet and romantic evening with a friend. Although I wasn't in a hurry I was in, fed, and out in ten minutes. It reminded me very much of a motorway filling station.

The Old Mill

Specialities of the day

Fresh Wardle Trout	£2.00
Wardle Estuary Oysters (½ doz)	£7.00
Grapefruit with White Port and Cinnamon	£2.00
Old Mill Pepper Steak	£5.95
Roast Shoulder of Sussex Lamb with Rosemary	£5.75
Fresh Fruit Salad	£2.00
Hot Black Cherries in Brandy	£2.00

+ full à la carte menu

Nashville Superburger Bar

1 Straight burger (2oz)	60p	
2 Big burger (4oz)	90p	
3 King-size burger (6oz)	£1.20	
4 Super burger (8oz)	£1.60	
5 Giant super burger (10oz)	£2.00	
6 Titanic burger (12oz)	£2.40	

All served in fresh, toasted buns with a choice of relishes.

Side orders of French fries:

7 Small	40p
8 Big	60p

Beverages:

9 Milk	30p
10 Selection of milkshakes	80p
11 Coffee	40p
12 Coca-cola	40p

Have a nice day!

Look at this

It was raining.   He took his umbrella.
He took his umbrella because it was raining.

It wasn't raining.   He took his umbrella.

Although Though Even though	it wasn't raining he took his umbrella.

Exercise
Now combine these sentences with 'because' or 'although'.

1 He didn't take the job. The salary was good.
2 Mark wasn't thirsty. He drank some milk.
3 They're afraid of flying. They flew to New York.
4 Sarah needed a new dress. She bought one.

Unit 58

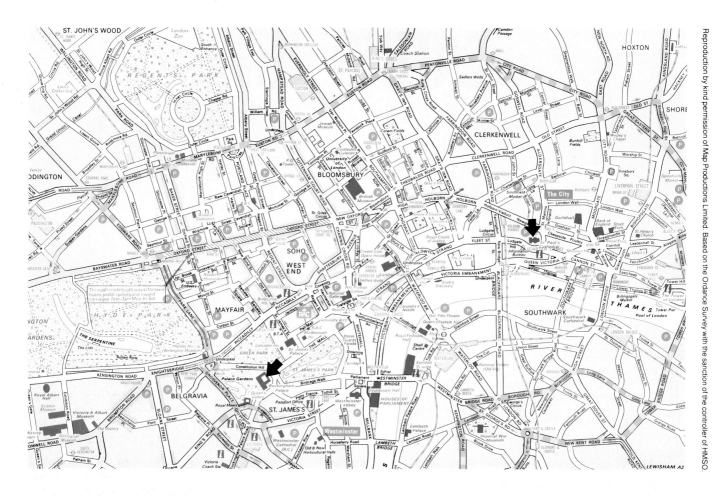

FINDING YOUR WAY AROUND

THE KNOWLEDGE

Becoming a London taxi driver isn't easy. In order to obtain a licence to drive a taxi in London, candidates have to pass a detailed examination. They have to learn not only the streets, landmarks and hotels, but also the quickest way to get there. This is called 'The Knowledge' by London cab drivers and it can take years of study and practice to get 'The Knowledge'. Candidates are examined not only on the quickest routes but also on the quickest routes at different times of the day. People who want to pass the examination spend much of their free time driving or even cycling around London, studying maps and learning the huge street directory by heart.

Monty Hunter is taking the examination now. Listen to the examiner's question and try to follow Monty's directions on the map of London.

Examiner OK, Monty. Ready? You're outside Buckingham Palace and you've just picked up a passenger who wants to go to St Paul's Cathedral. It isn't the rush-hour. Use the most direct route.

Monty I'd go straight along the Mall, round the one-way system at Trafalgar Square, and turn into Northumberland Avenue. I'd turn left along the Embankment and carry on as far as Blackfriars Bridge, turn left into New Bridge Street, then right at Ludgate Circus and up Ludgate Hill to St Paul's.

Exercise 1
Now practise with a partner. Point out your departure point on the map, state your destination and ask your partner to direct you.

Unit 59

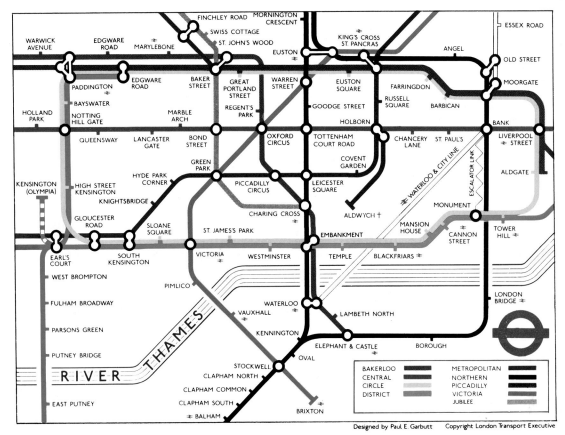

Designed by Paul E. Garbutt   Copyright London Transport Executive

THE UNDERGROUND

Travelling on the London underground (the 'tube') presents few difficulties for visitors because of the clear colour-coded maps. It is always useful to have plenty of spare change with you because there are often long queues at the larger stations. If you have enough change you can buy your ticket from a machine. You will find signs which list the stations in alphabetical order, with the correct fares, near the machines. There are automatic barriers which are operated by the tickets. You should keep the ticket, because it is checked at the destination.

Listen to these people talking about the underground map, and follow their routes on the map.

Peter and Susan have just arrived at Victoria.

Peter Right. We've got to get to Baker Street. Can you see it?

Susan Yes, it's up here. It looks easy enough. We just take the Victoria line to Green Park, then change to the Jubilee line. That goes straight there. It's only the second stop from Green Park.

Laura is at the enquiry office at King's Cross.

Laura Oh, excuse me. How do I get to King's Road, Chelsea. I mean, which is the nearest tube station?

Clerk You want Sloane Square. Take a look at this map. The best way is to take the Victoria line, that's this light blue one, as far as Victoria Station. Then you'll have to change. When you get to Victoria, follow the signs for the Circle and District lines, they're on the same platform. Then take the first westbound train. It doesn't matter which one it is. Sloane Square's the next stop.

Laura Thank you very much indeed.

Simon and Elizabeth are at Waterloo.

Simon Where's a map?

Elizabeth There's one over here. They said the hotel was near Russell Square. Can you see it?

Simon Yes, it's up here. In the top right of the map. Look, I reckon we should take the Bakerloo as far as Piccadilly Circus, then change to the Piccadilly line, that's the dark blue one. It's only four stops to Russell Square.

Elizabeth Are you sure that's the quickest way? We could take the Northern line (it's the black one) to Leicester Square, and join the Piccadilly line there.

Simon There's not much in it, really. We might as well take the Northern. Have you got any change for the ticket machine?

Exercise 2

Practise with a partner. Give directions from:
1 Sloane Square to Marble Arch
2 Baker Street to Russell Square
3 Waterloo to Paddington
4 Victoria to Great Portland Street
5 Pimlico to Russell Square
6 Great Portland Street to St Paul's

Exercise 3

Here are some famous London landmarks with their nearest tube stations. Make conversations about getting to them from: **a** Sloane Square, **b** St Paul's, **c** Marble Arch.
1 Buckingham Palace (St James's Park)
2 British Museum (Russell Square)
3 National Gallery (Trafalgar Square)
4 Houses of Parliament (Westminster)
5 Tower of London (Tower Hill)
6 Madame Tussaud's (Baker Street)

Exercise 4

Practise with a partner. State a departure point and destination. Your partner has to give you directions.

Unit 59

Good evening, and here is the Eight O'Clock News.

Five thousand people marched through the streets of Chesilworth today protesting against plans for a new international airport near the town. Although there was such a large number of demonstrators, there was no trouble. The demonstrators marched to the town hall, where a public enquiry into the plans was taking place, and handed in a petition to the chairman of the enquiry. A new airport is needed because the other airports in the London area are overcrowded. Several sites for the new airport have been suggested, and Chesilworth was considered because it is near both a major motorway and a railway line. Although it was a protest march, there was almost a carnival atmosphere, and both demonstrators and police remained good-humoured.

Families were evacuated from four streets in the centre of Glasgow today, because of a gas explosion. The explosion occurred at ten a.m. in a deserted house in Mickle Street. Gas Board officials believe that the explosion was due to leaking gas. The house had been empty for several months, and they suspect that a gas main had cracked because of vibration from road-works in the street. Windows 100 metres away were broken by the blast. The police have forbidden anyone to enter the area until the Gas Board has completed tests.

Air-sea rescue helicopters from RAF Sopworth were called out after a yacht capsized in a storm off the Devon coast. Despite high seas the helicopters lowered rescue teams to try and save the crew. Two men and a girl were pulled to safety. Unfortunately, the other two crewmembers died in spite of the rescue team's efforts. One was lost at sea. The other was rescued and taken to hospital, but was dead on arrival. The coastguard had warned small boats to stay in the harbour, but the yacht, the 'Neptune III' from Poole, had set out for France despite the warnings.

Fernside Engineering announced today that they are closing their plant in Tadworth. Three hundred jobs will be lost because of the closure, which is due to a sharp decline in orders for their products. There have been

THE EIGHT O'CLOCK NEWS

rumours for several weeks that the plant might be closed, and in spite of lengthy discussions between unions and management, closure became inevitable because of the cancellation of several major orders. As well as the three hundred redundancies at Tadworth, union leaders predict further redundancies in the area, in firms which supply Fernside Engineering with components.

Reports are coming in of a 100 mph car chase through the roads of Hampshire. Police disturbed a gang of men who were breaking into a chemist's in Lyndford. However, the men escaped in a stolen Jaguar saloon, and the police chased them through the New Forest at high speed. The Jaguar was forced off the road near Bransley. The men were armed with shot-guns, but nevertheless police-officers chased them across a field. Several shots were fired. Fortunately, however, no one was injured, and the men were taken into custody.

Brighton Belle XIV, a four-year-old Dalmatian bitch, became the 'Supreme Champion Dog' at Cruft's Dog Show in London. There were almost 10,000 dogs on show, worth around £8,000,000. There were 120 judges looking at 144 different breeds of dog. Brighton Belle XIV is expected to earn up to £100,000 in breeding and advertising fees.

And lastly, sport. Eastfield United are through to the next round of the European Cup after an exciting match in Scotland. Dunromin Rangers scored twice in the first half, and although Eastfield were two down at half-time, they went on to win with a hat trick by Trevor Franklin in the second half. Towards the end of the second half, Franklin was limping because of a knee injury, but nevertheless managed to score the winning goal one minute from time. The game was stopped twice because of fighting in the crowd, but in spite of the trouble, and in spite of the appalling weather, both teams played well. Viewers will be able to see highlights of the match after the news.

Look at this

It was snowing so she wore a coat.

or

| She wore a coat | because it was snowing. |
| | because of the snow. |

or

| Because it was snowing, | she wore a coat. |
| Because of the snow, | |

It was snowing, but she didn't wear a coat.

or

She didn't wear a coat	although it was snowing.
	in spite of / the snow.
	despite

or

Although it was snowing,	she didn't wear a
In spite of / the snow,	coat.
Despite	

It was difficult, but he managed to do it.

or

| It was difficult. | However, | he managed |
| | Nevertheless, | to do it. |

or

| It was difficult. He managed to | however. |
| do it | nevertheless. |

Exercise

Now write the news for today.

ALL THE GOOD NEWS

THE SUNDAY TIMES   NOVEMBER 12

Our news present to Charles

Prince Charles, speaking at a Press Awards lunch, once asked why newspapers only printed the bad news. 'Why don't they, for a change, tell us how many jumbo jets landed safely at Heathrow Airport?' Later the same year a leading British newspaper published a column of 'good news' as a birthday present for Prince Charles. Here are some of the news items.

♣ Last week 330 jumbo jets landed or took off without incident at Heathrow, the world's leading international airport, with 20 million international passengers, which is double the number at New York's Kennedy Airport, the world's second busiest international terminal.

♣ Approximately 12,200 happy, gurgling babies were delivered to British mothers last week.

♣ 92 per cent of the first class mail was also delivered on time.

♣ The government received its first chunk of petroleum revenue tax last week – £176 million from BP's successful 'Forties' oil-field. The first oil from the Ninian group of oil-fields was moving through the pipeline towards its terminal in the Shetland Islands, part of the riches undreamed of a decade ago of 1,100,000 barrels a day from North Sea oil.

♣ The battle to clean up the River Thames is being won. Species of fish, which even ten years ago could not have survived in the polluted water, are being caught in increasing numbers.

♣ About 6,500 couples emerged happily from churches and registry offices.

♣ Last week was 'National Tree Planting Week'. Thousands of seedlings were planted.

♣ British Rail carried two million passengers each working day with 88 per cent of express trains arriving within ten minutes of schedule.

♣ Canterbury Cathedral was con-ducting services in its 798th year.

♣ At the Houses of Parliament, where Big Ben was telling the right time, the House of Commons resumed its 306th Parliament since 1213.

♣ Britain's ladies won the Wightman Cup tennis tournament.

♣ Two women clerks won equal pay for 14,000 young women at Lloyds Bank.

♣ Despite the example of the Church of England, which is still refusing to ordain women priests, Liz Beal, aged 13, won permission to play Rugby League Football.

♣ Five children at the Great Ormond Street Hospital for Sick Children were successfully operated on for congenital heart defects – some of the 2,000 babies now benefiting from the treatment each year.

♣ Britain's gold and currency reserves amounted to £15,977 million, and this year we have repaid foreign loans to the value of £3,500 million.

♣ Sotheby's, the auctioneers, auctioned a cello for a record £144,000.

♣ By the end of this year, 30,000 home students will have been awarded degrees by the Open University, which operates through post, television, radio, and short summer courses to enable people to get a university degree at home.

♣ Bovis, the construction company, won a £15 million contract to build three schools in Saudi Arabia. 47 British companies were exhibiting at a trade fair in Peking, and over 200 at a trade fair in Mexico City.

♣ Even farmers were smiling last week. At the beginning of the good weather they were able to bring in a record cereal harvest with the minimum effort. Since then, there has been no rain and autumn ploughing and sowing is going wonderfully well.

PS: The death rate from suicide is going down.

Exercise 1
Find words in the text which mean:
1 A period of ten years.
2 A place where people can marry without a religious ceremony.
3 A young newly grown tree.
4 A programme of pre-arranged times.
5 A contest of skill between a number of players.
6 Groups of animals or plants (which are able to breed together).
7 A formal legal agreement.
8 Firms which sell goods at a public sale to the person who offers most money.
9 The collection of fruit, grain or vegetables made by a farmer.
10 A standard measurement for oil.

Exercise 2
Find expressions which mean:
1 twice as many as
2 with no unusual occurrences
3 showing the time correctly
4 with as little work as possible

Exercise 3
There are five examples of the use of 'to win'. What are they?

Discussion points

❝When a dog bites a man, that is not news, but when a man bites a dog that is news.❞

❝No news is good news.❞

What do you think these sayings mean? Discuss.
Prince Charles said that newspapers always print the bad news. Is that true?
Why do you think newspapers might concentrate on 'bad' news?
Would you buy a newspaper which only reported 'good' news? Why? Why not?
Did you hear the news yesterday? What was it? Was it all bad?
Give some examples of 'good' news.

Unit 61

THE ANNUAL DINNER AND DANCE

Every year, 'Continental Computers' holds an annual dinner and dance, to which all employees and their husbands and wives are invited. It is the only time of the year when all the employees get together socially.

Christopher Simpson is a young accounts clerk. He's speaking to Edward Wallis, the Chief Personnel Officer.

Chris Mr Wallis? Can I buy you a drink?

Mr W Oh, that's very kind of you, Christopher. I'll have a scotch, a large one.

Chris Ice?

Mr W No, no, no. Just a splash of soda, please. Thank you.

Chris Er ... I wanted to ask you what was happening about the job in Sheffield.

Mr W It's being advertised next week. Are you interested?

Chris I might be. I really don't know what to do. I'm quite happy here, but it would be a promotion. Do you think I should apply?

Mr W Why not? There's no harm in trying. I'll tell you what to do. Pop up and see me on Monday, and I'll tell you what I can about the job.

Martin Webber is a computer programmer. He's at the dance with his wife, Melanie.

Martin Melanie, do you have to flirt with Philip every time we come to a dance?

Melanie We were only dancing. There's no need to get jealous.

Martin I saw what he was doing! He was whispering to you!

Melanie Oh, Martin! You don't know what you're talking about. He had to speak into my ear because of the music! How many drinks have you had?

Martin Oh, come on! That's got nothing to do with it!

Melanie Do you want to hear what he said?

Martin I don't care what he said, I...

Melanie He was asking me what he should buy for his wife's birthday, that's all!

Jacqueline Dibben works in the Marketing Department. She's just met Fiona Johnson, who's in charge of advertising.

Fiona Ah, Jacky! So you're back from New York.

Jacky Yes, Fiona. I've been doing market research there.

Fiona I know. How did you get on?

Jacky Well, what I saw in the States astonished me ... really! I think there'll be a lot of demand for our new 2CL home computer.

Fiona That's very interesting.

Jacky Yes. What I heard was very encouraging. We've got just what they're looking for.

Sir Joseph Lennox is the Managing Director. He's just run into Alex Fielding, one of the union representatives.

Sir Joseph Good evening, Mr Fielding.

Alex Good evening, Sir Joseph.

Sir Joseph Did you get my message about the meeting on Monday?

Alex Yes, I did, but I'm still not absolutely sure what the meeting's about. Not bad news, I hope.

Sir Joseph No, no. Don't worry. It's good news, in fact. What we'd like to do is expand production of the new home computer. Either we'll have to increase overtime working or take on new staff.

Alex That sounds promising. What we'll need to know is exactly how much more work will be created.

Sir Joseph I'll give you all the facts and figures on Monday. But let's forget about all that now. We don't want to talk shop all night, do we? That's not what this evening's all about. Another drink?

Alex Please.

Kelly's a secretary and Teresa works in the Data Processing Department.

Kelly Hey, Teresa. Wasn't that Neil Pincher you were dancing with?

Teresa Yes. Do you know what he asked me?

Kelly No.

Teresa He invited me out for dinner.

Kelly You're not going, are you?

Teresa No fear! I've heard all about him. I wouldn't go out with him if he was the last man on earth.

Kelly So what did you say?

Teresa What I wanted to say was, 'Go to hell', but I just told him I was busy.

Look at this

I don't know *what* to do.
I'll tell you *what* I can.
What I saw astonished me.

THE APPRENTICE

It's Alan Newman's first day in his first job. He's started work in an electrical components factory. The Personnel Officer, Mrs Vaughan, is introducing him to Bert Hogg, who has worked there for thirty years.

Mrs Vaughan Alan, this is Bert, Bert Hogg. You'll be working with him.

Alan Morning, Mr Hogg.

Bert You can call me Bert, son. Don't worry. I'll show you what to do.

Mrs Vaughan Can I leave him with you then, Bert?

Bert Oh, yes, Mrs Vaughan. I'll look after him. Follow me, son.

Bert Right, son. Any questions?

Alan Er . . . yes. Where can I leave my coat and things?

Bert There's a row of lockers over there. It doesn't matter which one you use. Take whichever one you want.

Alan Oh, thanks. And I've got my National Insurance card here. Who should I give it to?

Bert You should have given it to Mrs Vaughan. I don't suppose she asked you for it. Just take it up to the office. You can give it to whoever is there. They'll pass it on to her.

Alan When can I do that?

Bert It doesn't matter really. Take it whenever you like, lad, but I'll give you a tip. Don't take it during the tea-break. You know what I mean?

Alan Right. Thanks.

Alan Oh, another thing. Where can I leave my motor-bike?

Bert There's plenty of room in the car-park. Just don't put it in a numbered space. They're reserved for the directors' cars. But apart from that, you can leave it wherever there's room. Come on, I'll show you where you'll be working. Right, this is our bench. Just watch me, and do whatever I tell you, OK?

Alan OK.

Bert First of all, you can clean these tools. There's a bottle of white spirit on the shelf.

Alan All right. Is there any special way of doing it?

Bert Eh? Special way? No, son, no. Clean them however you want. There's no special way.

10.30.

Bert Oi! Alan, you can stop work for a bit. It's time for the tea-break.

Alan Thanks.

Bert Don't thank me, son. You've done well. You'll need a cup of tea. Oh, look . . . after the tea-break I want you to go to the stores and get me a few things. Is that all right?

Alan Oh, yes. I'll get whatever you want.

Bert Good lad. Now, I'll need a tin of striped paint, a rubber hammer and a glass nail, a left-handed screw-driver, and a bucket of steam. Oh, and tell them Bert sent you.

At the stores.

Alan Morning.

Storeman Morning.

Alan I've come to get a tin of striped paint.

Storeman A what? What ever are you talking about, son?

Alan A tin of striped paint. I want a tin of striped paint.

Storeman Who ever told you to come and get that?

Alan Bert . . . er, Bert Hogg.

Storeman Oh, Bert Hogg! What colour stripes would you like, son?

Alan I'm not sure. Perhaps I'd better ask him.

Storeman I suppose he asked you to get a right-handed screw-driver, as well.

Alan No, he wants a left-handed one.

Storeman Just stop and think for a minute, lad! Just stop and think!

Exercise 1

A What do you fancy doing this evening?

B *I don't mind. Whatever you like.*

1 Well where shall we go then?
2 How shall we go there?
3 Which would you prefer, bus or taxi?
4 When do you think we should leave?
5 Which pub would you like to go to?
6 What shall we have to drink?
7 Where shall we go for a meal?
8 Who shall we invite to the party?
9 What shall we give them to eat?

Exercise 2

A What shall I do with these old newspapers?

B *It doesn't matter. Do whatever you want.*

1 Which of these books can I borrow?
2 Who shall I give my ticket to?
3 When can I come to see you?
4 How should I do it?
5 Where can I park my car?

Exercise 3

A He's talking about something. Nobody knows what!

B *What ever is he talking about?*

1 They found out about it. Nobody knows how!
2 She's been somewhere. Nobody knows where!
3 He gave it to someone. Nobody knows who!
4 She found time to do it. Nobody knows when!
5 They jumped in the river. Nobody knows why!

A CHANGE FOR THE BETTER?

Newspapers and magazines are full of advertisements which try to persuade people to change their appearance in one way or another. Look at these advertisements, and discuss them.

Classified

EARS PIERCED

WHILE YOU WAIT

Painless procedure. No appointment necessary. Reasonable rates. Large selection of studs and earrings. Also nose piercing by arrangement.

Pinner Jewellery Centre,
Pinner, Middlesex

BE TALLER!

with our custom-made shoes. We can add up to 5cm to your height . . . and only you will ever know. Our unique design ensures both comfort and confidence.

**Platform Two
Solihull**

Sparta Health and Slimming Clinic

★ Gymnasium ★ Programmes of Exercise ★ Sauna
★ Massage ★ Solarium ★ Dietary Advice ★ Latest
Electronic Slimming Aids

Mrs B of Scarborough writes:

"I lost 15 kilos in 12 weeks. I feel younger, fitter and happier . . . and I owe it all to my local Sparta Clinic. I am a new woman . . ."

Sparta Clinics – in 30 cities and towns throughout Britain. Consult your local telephone directory.

Leo Rembrandt

TATTOO ARTIST
18 Victory Street, Portsmouth

Choose from a wide selection of traditional and modern designs and patterns. All kinds of lettering. Variety of colours. Quick, hygienic, almost painless method using an electric needle. Non-toxic dyes.

Anywhere, any size!

"Would you like a body like mine?"

I used to weigh 50 kilos until I discovered the Dynomatic system of body-building. Three years later I became "Mr Galaxy". Do yourself a favour!

**Write now to Ed Sampson,
P O Box 40, Gotham, USA.**

Bald? Balding? Receding? Bald patches? Premature hair loss? Greying?

BEFORE   AFTER

**Look years younger! Contact the
BRYNNER HAIR ADVISORY CENTRE
Tel: 327184**

Telephone us or call in and arrange an immediate free consultation in complete confidence! Treatment to suit every pocket.

☐ Hair restorer ☐ Vitamin & mineral supplements ☐ Toupees ☐ Hair replacement and addition ☐ Hair transplants (relocation of healthy. growing hairs to thinning and bald areas)

Harley Manor Private Clinic

Can arrange cosmetic surgery by plastic surgeons of international repute. Cosmetic surgery can often restore lost confidence.

★ **DISFIGURING SCARS CAN BE REMOVED** ★
RESHAPING ★ **FACIAL CONTOURING** ★

Our clients have included leading figures from the worlds of entertainment, politics and business.

You should consult your own medical practitioner before contacting us.

Full details available from Sheila Skinner, Dept. B, Harley Manor, Nazelton.

New super tooth make-up

Blanche as used by models and T.V. quizmasters! Discoloured teeth, dentures and fillings can now be given a sparkling white finish with **Blanche**. Simple to use – brushed on in seconds. Touch up every 2/3 days. Laboratory tested!

Blanche Products, London NW4

Do you lack confidence?

Are you afraid of speaking to people? making dates? eating out? going to parties? travelling?

Do you feel inferior? blush? stammer? tremble?

Write for our introductory booklet (sent in a plain, sealed envelope), "The will and the way".

**THE ROOKER INSTITUTE,
Conman St., London W1**

Wear glasses?

Do you play sports? Are you fed up with wearing spectacles?

Have you considered contact lenses?
The new soft lenses are comfortable and easier to wear.

Consult your local optician, or send for information to British Optical Council, Newton House, Devizes.

GOING TO THE DOCTOR'S

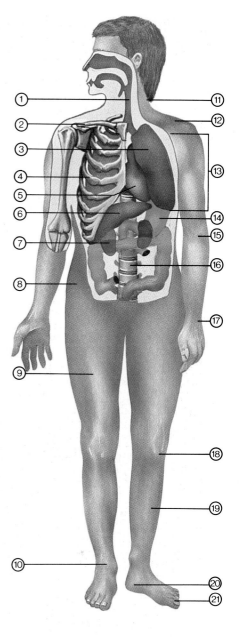

Exercise 1

List as many words as you can about:
a illness
b medical treatment
c parts of the body.

Listen to the conversation and tick any words in your list that are used in the conversation.

Craig Williams has gone to see Dr Casey at the Health Centre. He's in his surgery now.

Wayne fell off his bicycle. He's in the casualty department at the local hospital. Dr Singh is examining him.

Doctor Hello, Wayne, isn't it? You've had a bit of a fall. What were you doing? Going too fast?

Wayne Yes, doctor. I fell off going round a corner.

Doctor You'd better get undressed then, and we'll take a look at you. Mm. That's a nasty cut. I'll have to put a couple of stitches in that.

Wayne I've got a cut here too, doctor.

Doctor It looks worse than it is. It's only a graze. The nurse will clean it up for you. It'll sting, but that's all. Now, does it hurt anywhere else?

Wayne I've got a pain in my arm. It's very sore, and it feels stiff.

Doctor Well, there's nothing broken, but you've bruised your shoulder. It'll be sore for a few days. Now, did you bang your head at all?

Wayne Yes, I did. I fell onto the bike. But it doesn't hurt now.

Doctor Did you feel dizzy?

Wayne No, not at all.

Doctor Look up there, I'm just going to shine this light in your eye. No, that's fine. I'll just do the stitches, and the nurse will put a dressing on it. Then you can go home.

Mrs Mallard has gone to see Dr Gillespie, her family doctor.

Mrs Mallard Good morning, doctor.

Doctor Ah, good morning, Mrs Mallard. What can I do for you this time?

Mrs Mallard It's those pills, doctor. They don't seem to be doing me any good.

Doctor Really? What's wrong?

Mrs Mallard What isn't wrong with me, doctor! It's old age, I suppose.

Doctor You're doing very well, Mrs Mallard! You'll live to be a hundred!

Mrs Mallard I've got this terrible cough, doctor, and I've still got that rash on my hands. And the backache! I can hardly walk sometimes. You don't think it's that legionnaire's disease, do you? I've been reading about it in the paper.

Doctor No, no . . . no chance of that. You're very fit for your age.

Mrs Mallard Pardon? Anyway, I've nearly finished the old pills, doctor. Can you give me a different colour next time?

① throat	⑧ hip	⑮ elbow
② collar bone	⑨ thigh	⑯ spine
③ lung	⑩ ankle	⑰ wrist
④ rib	⑪ neck	⑱ knee
⑤ heart	⑫ shoulder	⑲ shin
⑥ liver	⑬ chest	⑳ heel
⑦ kidney	⑭ stomach	㉑ toe

Exercise 2

Rosemary Key wants to take out a life insurance policy. The insurance company has sent her to see a doctor for a check up. This is part of the form he has to complete.

Practise their conversation. (*Can I take your . . .?/Have you ever had . . .?/Have you been vaccinated against . . .?* etc.)

FRIARY INSURANCE NORWICH   CONFIDENTIAL

Name	Children	Address ....
Marital status	Occupation	....
Date of birth	....	....

Measurements

Height	Chest (a) normal	Waist ....
Weight	(b) expanded	Hips ....
Blood pressure	Pulse rate	Vision ....

Medical history (*please give approximate dates where possible*)

Measles	**Vaccinations and inoculations**	*Please give details of any hospital*
Mumps	Polio	*treatment or operations (not including*
Rubella (German measles)	Scarlet fever	*normal pregnancy)*
Chicken-pox	Diphtheria	
Whooping cough	Whooping cough	
Other serious illnesses (*give details*	Measles	
below)	Tetanus	
....	....	
....	....	

A MESSAGE TO THE STARS

Our planet Earth is one of nine planets revolving around the Sun, a fairly small and ordinary star, which lies in the outer areas of the Milky Way galaxy. There are about 250 billion stars in our galaxy, and billions of galaxies in the universe. People have always wondered about the possibility of intelligent life forms on other planets. In recent years this has become serious scientific speculation. Some scientists believe that there must be large numbers of stars with planets which could support living intelligent beings. Perhaps we shall never know. The nearest star is 4.3 light years away. A light year is the distance covered by light (travelling at almost 300,000 kilometres a second) in one year. It would take the fastest Earth spacecraft about 40,000 years to reach the nearest star.

For a number of years radio telescopes have been trying to pick up signals from outer space, so far without success. There are, however, millions of possible radio frequencies, and there is no reason why a completely alien civilization should not use a different type of communication, such as X-rays or even a type of wave we have not yet discovered. Suppose contact were made with beings 300 light years away. By the time we had sent our reply, and received their response, the earth would be 600 years older. It would be an interesting, but rather slow-moving, conversation!

Pioneer 10

The first man-made object to leave our solar system was the Pioneer 10 spacecraft. It was launched from Cape Kennedy on March 3rd, 1972. It was designed to pass close to the planet Jupiter and then continue into deep space. A gold plaque, about 15cm by 22cm, was placed on the spacecraft. On the plaque is a dia-

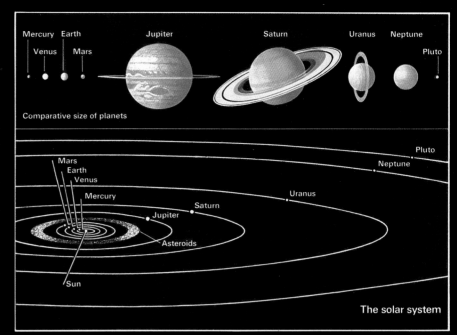

Comparative size of planets

The solar system

gram showing the solar system, and its location in the galaxy. There is also a drawing of a naked man and woman, standing in front of a picture of the spacecraft. The man's right hand is raised in a gesture of friendship. It is unlikely, however, that the plaque will ever be seen again. If it were found by an alien civilization it seems improbable that they would be able to interpret it.

The Voyager mission

Every 175 years the large outer planets – Jupiter, Saturn, Uranus, and Neptune – are in such a position that a spacecraft from Earth can fly past all of them. The two Voyager spacecraft were launched in 1977 to photograph and investigate these planets. Voyager I passed Jupiter in December 1978 and reached Saturn in November 1980. It sent back dramatic pictures of the rings of Saturn and discovered previously unknown moons. It then left the solar system. Voyager II was designed to reach Saturn in

July 1981, Uranus in January 1986 and Neptune in August 1989 before leaving the solar system to travel silently through space forever.

As well as a pictorial plaque, Voyager II carries a gold sprayed disc. The disc contains greetings in 60 languages, 140 photographs, and one and a half hours of music and songs, ranging in style from Beethoven and Mozart to the Beatles and Chuck Berry.

Exercise 1
Imagine you could send objects, weighing up to five kilos which would give an impression of civilization on Earth. This would include a record and a video tape with photographs and film. What would you choose to send and why?

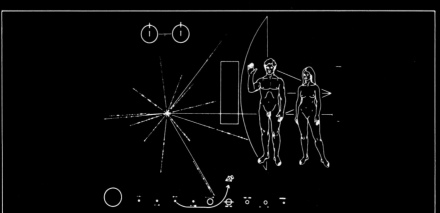

Exercise 2
Space research costs billions of dollars. Some people think that the money would be better spent on more practical projects here on Earth. What do you think?

IT'S ABOUT TIME

Janet and Bruce live in London. Janet's younger sister, Pam, who lives in Edinburgh, is flying down to spend the weekend with them.

Janet Bruce, I think it's time to go and meet Pam at the airport.
Bruce Oh, no, we've no need to hurry. There's plenty of time. It's only half past eight. There won't be much traffic at this time of night.
Janet You never know, and I think your watch must be slow. I make it 8.40, and you'll have to stop for petrol. I'd sooner we were too early than too late!
Bruce It'll take her a while to get her luggage.
Janet Oh, come on, Bruce! It's time we were leaving. We can always have a coffee at the airport. Anyway, I like watching people at the airport.
Bruce I'd rather see the end of the football match, but never mind, we'd better go.

Bruce Janet! Hold on a minute, there's the phone.
Janet You haven't got time to answer it now. Ignore it.
Bruce No, I'd better see who it is. It might be important. Bruce McGregor speaking ... oh, Pam, we were just on our way to fetch you. Oh, no! Hold on, I'll get Janet.

Janet Pam! Where are you?
Pam I'm still in Edinburgh. The flight's been delayed.

Janet You caught us just in time. We were about to leave for the airport.
Pam I know, Bruce said so. I'm glad I phoned. You'd have had a long wait otherwise.
Janet When will you be leaving, do you think?
Pam Oh, not for an hour at least. Look, don't bother to come out to the airport.
Janet It's no trouble. We'll meet you.
Pam No, I'd rather you didn't. Honestly.
Janet Now, don't be silly, Pam. We'll collect you.
Pam No, Janet, I'd rather get a taxi.
Janet We'll be there, Pam! See you later.

Bruce It's nearly 12.30.
Janet Well, we couldn't let her find her own way. Not at this time of night!
Bruce She knows how to look after herself. That plane landed half an hour ago. It's about time she was here.
Janet It always takes ages to get your luggage.
Bruce I know. It's about time they did something about it. Last time, it took me longer than the flight!
Janet Oh, Bruce, there she is!
Bruce About time, too.
Janet Pam! Pam! Over here!

Bruce I'll go and bring the car round. I won't be long.
Janet Well, Pam, what would you rather do tomorrow morning, lie in or go shopping?

Pam This morning, you mean! I'd rather go shopping, but there's no need for you to get up and come with me. I'd rather you had a lie in. You must be tired out!
Janet I am a bit tired. But I'll meet you for lunch. There's a new restaurant just off Kensington High Street. Do you think you'll be able to find your way there?
Pam Oh, Janet! It isn't as if this were my first visit to London! You can tell me where it is in the morning.

Look at this

I'd	rather sooner	go there.	

I'd	rather sooner	you he she we they	went there. didn't go there.

It's time to go.

It's (about) time	we left. we were leaving.

It isn't as	if though	this were my first visit. he didn't know.

Exercise 1
The baggage handling is slow. They should do something about it.
It's about time they did something about it.
Continue.
1 It's late. We should go to the airport.
2 She's getting tired. She should go to bed.
3 He coughs a lot. He should stop smoking.
4 The windows are dirty. We should clean them.
5 The bus is late. It should be here.
6 He's bored. He should find an interesting job.

Exercise 2
Are you going to do it?
No, I'd rather not do it. I'd rather you did it.
Continue.
1 Are you going to write to her?
2 Would you like to drive?
3 Do you want to ask him?
4 Would you like to choose?
5 Do you want to arrange it?
6 Are you going to see the manager?

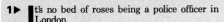

1▶ It's no bed of roses being a police officer in London.

When people need help they're only too happy to call you. But just you turn up when it doesn't suit them and what you can get called isn't fit to print.

After a while, however, the experience can become very printable indeed.

Published recently was a paperback written by a south London copper called "Policeman's Progress."

2▶ Here are some random quotes, by Police Constable Harry Cole:

"It is one of the few occupations left in present day society where a person can arrive for work ... and have no idea what the day will bring. It could be an accident, a murder... an armed robbery, arson or a request for directions. It could be an explosion, a false alarm or a drunk."

"I was asked about holidays, treatment for budgies, wallpapering, social security, conservation, contraception, politics and prison visits. I was called upon to chastise drunken husbands (occasional success), errant wives (hundred percent failure), wayward kids and obstinate grandparents."

"I received anonymous threatening letters (I recognised the writing), anonymous threatening phone calls (I recognised the voice), and an anonymous cake for my... birthday (it was stale)."

"I was invited to christenings, weddings and divorces (often in that order, particularly with the very young)."

"CLEAR OFF FUZZ. THIS IS A PRIVATE QUARREL."

"SHE'S ONLY 3 YEARS OLD. SHE'S BEEN MISSING FOR 3 HOURS."

"OFFICER, YOU DID NOT SEE ME GO THROUGH A RED LIGHT."

"THANK GOD YOU'VE ARRIVED OFFICER. THE DRIVER IS LOSING BLOOD."

"YOU ONLY STOP ME 'COS I'M BLACK."

"WATCH IT COPPER, I'VE GOT A KNIFE."

"TWO MEN HAVE JUST BROKEN INTO MY SHOP."

"MY HANDBAG HAS BEEN SNATCHED."

Could you put up with a calling like ours?

"I rarely completed a Christmas duty without having to report a suicide, usually caused by loneliness."

"The bodies, dogs, demos, drunks and fights; the villains and the victims; the brutal, the gentle, the cowardly and the brave; the haters, the lovers and the just plain indifferent ... One day I shall have to live without them; it won't be easy."

3▶ Any police officer in London could tell you a similar story. But the question it would raise is the same.

What kind of person measures up to such a job?

It isn't enough for a man to reach the required minimum height of 172 cm (5'8"). Or for a woman to make 162 cm (5'4").

Regardless of your height you're obviously no good if you don't have the stature for the job.

This means having a real concern for people. A real sense of fair play.

And a real sense of humour.

Qualities more valuable, in our view, than qualifications.

(If you have a few 'O' levels, fine. A university degree is no handicap either.

But best of all is a degree of common sense.)

If you're under 22 you'll earn £4,956 a year the day you join us.

If you're older you'll start at £5,919.

(What's more you'll pick up London Allowances of £1,482.)

You'll also get somewhere to live for free, if you need it.

Or we'll provide you with a tax-paid Rent Allowance up to £1,457 a year.

Believe us, you'll earn every penny of your pay.

Violent criminals, nasty accidents and freezing weather will all turn up when you least expect them.

But the reward you get as a human being for handling it all is compensation greater than any pay packet.

Still interested in being a Metropolitan Police Officer? You'll have to be over 18½ for a start.

If we haven't dimmed your enthusiasm, why not drop round our Careers Information Centre at New Scotland Yard in Victoria Street?

Or let us know your name, your age and your address and we'll send you the information you need.

The man to write to is The Chief Inspector, Metropolitan Police Careers Information Centre, Department OUP 15, New Scotland Yard, London SW1H 0BG.

Or you can phone us. Our number is 01-230 5215 and 5146.

Yours is one call we'll be especially pleased to get.

London needs people like you in the Metropolitan Police.

GOLD

Gold (Au) is a metallic chemical element. Atomic number 79. Atomic weight 197.2.

Since civilization began gold has been regarded as a symbol of power and wealth. In many societies gold was seen as a magic substance which could protect people against illness or evil spirits. It is the one material that has always been accepted in exchange for goods or services. Mankind never seems to have enough gold and the search for it has driven men mad. The need to search for gold has been compared to a disease, and is called 'gold fever'. In the Middle Ages men called 'alchemists' tried to manufacture gold from other metals. In spite of man's constant search for gold, the amount which has been produced since the beginning of time is only enough to make a solid block of eighteen cubic metres, the size of a large house.

Industrial uses

Because gold is untarnishable, workable, almost indestructible, durable, reflective and conductive, it has a number of industrial uses. About 10% of the annual production is used for industrial processes.

Gold is measured in troy ounces (31.1 grams). One ounce can be drawn into 80 kilometres of wire.

A single grain (0.065 grams) can be beaten down to make a sheet which would cover this page.

Between 20 and 30 ounces are needed for every jet engine.

Gold coatings, 0.000024 mm thick, are used to reflect heat from jet engine exhausts.

The windscreens of Concorde, other high speed aircraft, and some express trains have a gold electric heating element, 0.000005 mm thick, which is used to prevent icing.

Spacecraft are protected against radiation by a thin layer of the metal.

As it conducts electricity well and does not tarnish, gold is used extensively in computers and electric consumer goods.

For many years it has been blended with oils and applied as decoration to china and glass.

Because it is so reflective, it is employed in the manufacture of some roof tiles and glass.

Gold has always been prescribed for various ailments, and is used today to treat cancer and arthritis. It is used extensively in dentistry.

Decorative purposes

Because gold is valuable, bright, rare, attractive, durable and untarnishable it has always been used for decorative purposes.

Gold works of art were created by many of the great civilizations of the past, and may be seen in museums all over the world.

Since time immemorial gold has been coveted and desired. Until recent years it was worn only by the very rich and was considered the ultimate status symbol.

Gold jewellery is made to four standards, 22, 18, 14 and 9 carats. 18 carat gold is 18 parts gold out of 24, which is pure gold. That is, 18 carats is 75% pure gold. 24 carat gold is too soft for most purposes.

Gold jewellery includes rings, earrings, necklaces, bracelets, chains, pendants, armlets, anklets, medals, cuff-links, tie-pins, spectacle-frames and watches. It is also used to decorate pens, lighters, glasses, and books.

In traditional Indian cooking, gold flakes are used to decorate food and are consumed.

In Britain, gold is hallmarked, using a system which dates back to the twelfth century. There are five marks on gold which has been tested for quality in Britain.

The manufacturer's name is shown by a mark like this.

The crown shows that the article is gold, and has been hallmarked in the UK.

This shows the gold content. '375' is 9 carats (i.e. 37.5% pure gold).

The assay mark shows where it was tested. A leopard for London, an anchor for Birmingham, a rose for Sheffield, and a castle for Edinburgh.

A different letter is used for each year. 'J' was 1980.

Financial uses

The first gold coin was issued by King Croesus of Lydia in the sixth century BC. Today gold still plays an important part in the international monetary system.

About thirty years' production of gold is being held by central banks and monetary authorities, in spite of efforts to reduce its importance.

New deposits of gold are being found, and old mines are being reopened and it is likely that gold will always be valued as protection against inflation.

Gold can be bought by private investors in the forms of bars, coins and medals, as well as jewellery.

Gold production

Gold is found on all five continents, but 85% of the annual output of gold is produced by four countries:

South Africa 30 million oz
USSR   5½ million oz
Canada   4 million oz
USA   1½ million oz

In South Africa about three tonnes of gold-bearing rock have to be mined to produce each ounce of gold. Billions of tonnes of gold are suspended in the seas, but this gold is impossible to exploit at the moment.

Look at this
Gold *is used* for many purposes.
It *was produced* in ancient times.
Gold *has been used* for 6000 years.
New deposits *are being* found.
It *will be valued* in the future.
It *can be used* in industrial processes.
It *may be seen* in museums.
Three tonnes of rock *have to be mined* to produce an ounce of gold.

GOLD RUSH!

California

In 1848 gold was discovered at Sutter's Mill, about 100 miles east of San Francisco, and the first great goldrush began. When the news leaked out, farmers, trappers, lawyers, preachers, sailors, soldiers and school teachers rushed to California by whatever means they could. Within a year 100,000 people, only 8,000 of whom were women, had reached the coast of California. More than half of them had travelled overland across the American continent. 'Gold fever' began to spread. Settlements throughout the United States were deserted. Homes, farms and stores were abandoned as everybody raced for California. Many came by sea, and in July 1850 more than 500 ships were anchored in San Francisco Bay, many of which had been deserted by goldhungry sailors. A few people became fabulously rich, but it was a risky business. Law and order broke down. Even if a miner 'struck it rich' there were always those who would try to take it away: gamblers, outlaws, thieves and saloon keepers. Gold and silver were discovered in Nevada a few years later, and 'gold fever' was an important part of the colonization of the western United States.

Australia

The next major gold-rush occurred in 1851, when gold was struck in New South Wales, Australia. This led to another stampede and many rich finds were made. Other discoveries were made in Victoria and Kalgoorlie, Western Australia. In some places massive nuggets of gold were found accidentally, just lying about on the ground. The 'Welcome Stranger' nugget, which was found in 1869, weighed 78.37 kilos.

The Yukon

Perhaps the most difficult conditions were experienced by those prospectors who braved the Canadian winters to win gold from the Yukon and Klondike rivers. On August 16th 1896 three prospectors struck gold in Bonanza Creek, a tributary of the Klondike River, and then in a second creek which was named 'Eldorado'. In the Yukon, gold was obtained by washing gravel from river-beds, and soon as much as $800 worth of gold was being taken from a single pan of dirt. Within a year, Dawson had grown from nothing to a town of 30,000 people. Every man who entered the country had to carry a year's supply of food and mining equipment over steep and frozen mountain passes. To do this, each man had to carry 25 kilos of stores about 10 kilometres, leave it there, and return for another load. Therefore to move all his stores less than 80 kilometres, each man had to walk nearly 1500 kilometres. Horses and donkeys died in the ice and snow, but the men kept on going. It is estimated that of the 100,000 men who set out for the Klondike, fewer than 40,000 actually arrived. Only 4000 ever found gold, and very few of these became rich.

The rising price of gold in the late 1970s started a new rush to the Klondike. Dawson is still there, and 'Diamond Tooth Gertie's', the only legal gambling hall in Canada, remains in business. Just outside Dawson a mountain is actually being moved to find gold. The whole mountain is being washed down for gold-dust. It is believed to contain at least $80 million worth of gold.

South Africa

By the turn of the century gold had been found in South Africa and this laid the foundation for the world's largest goldmining industry. Today South Africa accounts for 70% of world gold production. Vast sums of money are being invested, and modern mining technology is being used to squeeze gold from the rock.

Twentieth-century gold-rush

New finds are being made in the Soviet Union, Saudi Arabia and the United States. The largest single mine in the world was discovered in Uzbekistan, USSR, in 1958. However, in spite of recent finds, modern day 'gold-rushes' are usually confined to speculation on the gold markets of Zurich, London and New York. At times of economic uncertainty investors rush hysterically to buy gold, and the price soars, often only to fall back again. Gold fever is in many ways irrational, but historically gold has always held its value, and it is likely that in an uncertain world, it will continue to do so.

Look at these expressions. What do you think they might mean?

A golden handshake.
The golden rule.
A golden age.
The golden gates.
A golden wedding.
A golden opportunity.
As good as gold.
Everything he touches turns to gold (or He's got the Midas touch).
All that glitters is not gold.
Don't kill the goose that lays the golden eggs.
A heart of gold.
A gold digger.
A gold disc.

THE CIRCUS IS COMING

Announcer This is RW2, Watermouth's own independent radio station. In the studio with me this morning is Sally Farnham, the daugher of circus owner, Bertie Farnham. Farnham's circus will be here in Watermouth for two weeks. That's right, isn't it, Sally?

Sally Yes, that's right. We open tomorrow for two weeks.

Announcer Has the circus arrived yet, Sally?

Sally No, no. Not yet. It's on the road somewhere between Sandpool and here.

Announcer I suppose there's a lot to be done between now and the first show.

Sally Yes, that's right. I've already been here for three days. There were all the advance arrangements to be made. It's like preparing for a small invasion.

Announcer What sort of things have you done?

Sally Oh, there are so many things to be done, you know. There are posters to be put up, newspaper ads to be arranged, casual labour to be hired and so on.

Announcer When will the circus actually arrive?

Sally In the next hour or so. The first trucks should be arriving any time now, and then the hard work really begins.

Announcer Most people love the circus, don't they? But not many realize how much work there is, do they?

Sally That's right. We'll be working all day and half the night. It's a bit like moving a small army. But, fingers crossed, by tomorrow morning everything will have been set up in time for the afternoon performance. Oh, there's the grand parade through the town centre at 11.30, so don't forget to come and see us.

Announcer Thank you, Sally, for coming in to talk to us. Now don't forget, folks. The grand circus parade will start from the pier at 11.30, go along the promenade, through the gardens and finish in Jubilee Park. Farnham's Circus will be in town for two weeks until 28th August. Now for some music.

Exercise 1
This is Sally's checklist of arrangements:
1 consult police about car parking (Wessex police)
2 arrange telephone lines (British Telecom)
3 connect water supply (Wessex Water Authority)
4 place ads (Watermouth Echo, Wessex Advertiser, Radio Watermouth)
5 order food supplies for animals (Wessex Meat Company)
6 arrange for fire inspection (Wessex Fire Brigade)

All of these things will have been done before the circus arrives. Make sentences.
A telephone line will have been arranged.
She'll have asked British Telecom.

Exercise 2
Sally's brother, Freddie Farnham, is in charge of the menagerie. This is his checklist:
1 unload animals
2 collect meat supplies
3 water animals
4 feed animals
5 check sanitary arrangements for animals
6 provide straw for animals

The animals have to be unloaded.
Make sentences.

Exercise 3
It's eleven o'clock on Sunday morning. There's a lot to be done. Sally's father, Bertie Farnham, is in charge of the arrangements.
1 erect big top
2 set up ticket office
3 park caravans
4 put up seating
5 erect cages
6 connect generators
7 put up safety net
8 set up high wire
9 put up trapezes
10 set up bandstand
11 place loudspeakers in tent
12 connect amplifiers
13 set up and connect lights
14 connect microphones
15 check everything

There's the big top to be erected.
Make sentences.

Unit 71

GETTING THINGS DONE

Anne Tim! That bathroom tap's still dripping. It's getting on my nerves! I thought you said you were going to fix it.

Tim Oh, yes ... the washer needs replacing.

Anne Why don't you replace it then?

Tim It's not as easy as that. I'll try and do it next week.

Anne But you said that last week.

Tim I know. I think you'd better phone for a plumber and get it done. I'm not really quite sure how to do it.

Exercise 1

Make conversations using the following:
1 That light's still broken/bulb holder/electrician
2 The stop light on my car's not working/bulb/take it to the garage
3 The record-player sounds terrible/stylus/take it to the shop
4 One of the rings on the cooker isn't working/element/electrician
5 The television reception's very poor/aerial/TV engineer

Adrian and Susannah are going on a touring holiday of France next week. They're taking their own car. Adrian always gives Susannah a lift to work. He's dropping her off outside her office.

Adrian Oh, Susannah! I won't be able to pick you up from work tonight. I'm having the car serviced. I thought we'd better have it done before we go.

Susannah That's all right. When are you collecting it?

Adrian Not till quarter to six. Why?

Susannah Well, I want to have my hair done before the holiday. I'll try and make an appointment to get it done after work. Then you can pick me up from the hairdresser's.

Adrian OK. Can you ring me at work and let me know what time?

Susannah Right, I'll call you later. Bye.

Exercise 2

HOLIDAY ADVICE

Before taking your car abroad, don't forget to:
- have a thorough service
- change the oil
- check the battery
- test the brakes
- check the tyres carefully and change if necessary
- have the lights adjusted for driving on the right

Adrian hasn't got time to do any of these things himself.
He's going to have the car serviced.
Make five more sentences.

Exercise 3

Susannah's going to have her hair done.
Make sentences with:
wash/shampoo/re-style/dye/cut/perm

Exercise 4

HOUSES FOR SALE

TERRACED house. Built 1872. 3 bedrooms. Needs some attention. Ideal for keen do-it-yourself enthusiast. Very reasonable price. Gatsby & Stahr, Estate Agents.

Look at the advertisement. This house is old, and is in very bad condition. Imagine you were interested in buying it. What do you think might need to be done to the house?
The house might need repainting.
Make a list.

Exercise 5

Listen to the conversation between an estate agent and Robin and Jean Harvey, who are looking at the house. Tick any items on your list that are mentioned in the conversation.

Exercise 6

When Robin and Jean are talking about the house, they mention some things that they could do themselves, and some things they would have to have done. Look at the chart below, and the example: they would have to have kitchen units put in. Listen to the conversation again, and complete the chart.

	Do it themselves	Have it done by someone else
Put in kitchen units		✓
Do kitchen ceiling		
Paint kitchen		
Rewire house		
Put in more power-points		
Redecorate lounge		
Convert small bedroom into bathroom		
Put toilet in bathroom		
Repair roof		
Put in central heating		
Double-glaze windows		

What could you do yourself, and what would you have done by someone else?

KEEPING FIT

MONDAY MARCH 30, 1981

QUESTIONNAIRE

1 Would you describe yourself as:
   □ Very fit   □ Average
   □ Quite fit   □ Unfit

   Do you think physical fitness is important?
   □ Yes   □ No

2 □ Do you ever get out of breath?
   □ Can you touch your toes (without bending your knees)?
   □ Can you run for 1 km?
   □ Can you hang from a bar, supporting your own weight for 20 seconds?

3 Does your daily routine involve any physical exertion?
   □ Yes   □ No

4 Do you take regular exercise?
   □ Yes   □ No

5 If you take regular exercise, how often do you take it?
   □ Every day   □ More than once a week
   □ Every other day   □ Once a week   □ Less

6 If you take regular exercise, in which of the following ways do you take it?
   □ Sport   □ Dance   □ Yoga
   □ Jogging   □ Cycling   □ Walking
   □ Swimming   □ Keep-fit exercises
   □ Other (What other ways? ....)

7 If you play a sport, is it:
   □ A team game   □ Amateur
   □ Competitive   □ Professional
   □ Organised

8 Do you possess any sports equipment?
   □ Yes   □ No

   If so, what? ....

9 Do you/Did you have to play any sports at school?
   □ Yes   □ No

   If so, which ones? ....

   How often? ....

10 Do you/Did you have P.E. (Physical Education) classes at school?
    □ Yes   □ No

    If so, how often? ....

11 Do you think sports or P.E. should be a compulsory part of the school curriculum?
    □ Yes   □ No

12 Why?/Why not? ....

Here are instructions for two keep-fit exercises:

Warming up exercise
Raise hands above head, feet apart. Bend forward slowly and touch ground in front of toes, then between feet. Don't worry if you can't reach the floor at first. Repeat 10 times the first day, and build up over 5 days to 20.

Exercise for bottom and hips
Sit on floor, legs outstretched, ankles crossed. Lean back slightly supporting weight on palms of hands. Lifting right arm above head, bend to left, keeping knees straight. Roll over until upper knee touches floor. Repeat to the right. Do it ten times in each direction. Cross ankles other way and repeat whole procedure.

If you do exercises, describe how to do them in detail. Get someone to follow your instructions. If you play a sport, describe the sport and briefly explain the rules, without mentioning the name of the sport. See if people can guess which sport you have described.

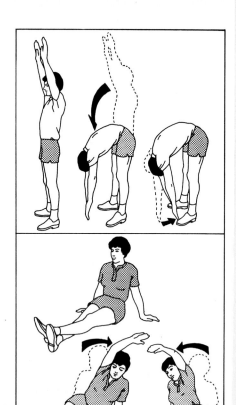

5,300 WIN MARATHON

One million people turned out to watch Britain's biggest-ever sporting event. The most amazing sporting event Britain has ever seen turned out to have 5,300 winners yesterday.

Around that number finished out of 6,700 who officially started in the first London Marathon and were cheered by a million people as they ran through the streets.

The first and last to complete the 26 miles and 385 yards symbolized in their different ways the spirit of the occasion.

At the front, Dick Beardsley from the United States and Inge Simonsen from Norway linked hands to run the last few yards and staged a dead heat for first place.

'What does it matter who wins?' said 24-year-old Beardsley. 'Every runner who finishes this race is a winner.' Some four hours later, last man home was the oldest competitor 78-year-old Bob Wiseman. 'I feel good. It's great to be alive,' he said.

The leaders made it an event of the highest athletic quality. At 2 hours, 11 minutes, 48 seconds, the joint winners ran the fastest marathon ever in Britain – and 142 runners finished under 2 hours 30 minutes.

Race director Chris Brasher, said: 'It went like a dream.'

St John Ambulance crews treated hundreds of runners for exhaustion, but the worst damage reported was a broken leg. 'We are surprised there weren't more casualties – everyone was very fit,' a spokesman said.

The drizzly conditions were ideal for marathon running – and competitors praised the cameraderie of those taking part and the encouragement given them by the spectators.

This aspect was summed up by 29-year-old jogger Ron Crowley, from Liverpool. Four miles from the finish he was on the point of quitting after stumbling to a halt.

Then, he said, he heard the crowd yelling out his number. 'No one has ever cheered like that for me before,' he said. 'They gave me heart to go on.'

DON'T PANIC

1 Don't forget to fasten your seat-belts!
2 Please do not leave your seat while the warning light is on.
3 May we remind passengers to read the emergency procedures.
4 Please do not smoke in the aisles or in the toilets.

5 Would you like to see the flight deck?

6 I'm busy now but I'll bring you a drink in a minute.

7 I'm afraid I can't give you another drink sir.

8 Here's the headset. Let me help you.

9 Please keep your belts fastened. We're going through turbulence.

10 Don't Panic!

11 Remove your shoes and proceed at once to the emergency exits.

12 Come on dear... you can make it! Just slide down the chute.

13 I'll have to push you.

Exercise 1

1 remind
She reminded them to fasten their seat-belts.
2 warn
She warned them not to leave their seats.
Continue.

3 remind	10 warn
4 tell	11 tell
5 invite	12 instruct
6 promise	13 order
7 help	14 urge
8 ask	15 force
9 refuse	

Exercise 2

Look at these sentences.
1 He said, 'No, no ... please don't shoot me.'
2 She said, 'Whatever you do, don't go to that dentist.'
3 He said, 'If I were you, I'd travel by train.'
4 He said, 'Would you like to come to a party on Saturday?'
5 She said, 'Don't forget to go to the bank today.'
6 The policeman said, 'Switch off the engine, and get out of the car.'
7 The old man said, 'Certainly not, I won't sell it at that price.'
8 She said, 'Don't worry. I'll definitely meet you at six o'clock.'
9 The attendant said, 'Would you mind moving your car?'
10 She said, 'I'm too busy now. Come back later.'

1 *He begged them not to shoot him.*

Continue, using these words:
refuse/ask/tell/warn/order/remind/advise/promise/invite.

Exercise 3

Practise with a partner (one is Student A, the other is Student B).

Student A	Student B
Ask B to meet you tonight.	Promise to meet A.
Advise B not to smoke so much.	Tell A to mind his own business.
Ask B to write a letter from your dictation.	Ask A to speak more slowly.
Invite B to a party.	Refuse politely.
Order B to be quiet.	Tell A not to talk to you like that.
Remind B to repay the money you lent him.	Promise to pay tomorrow.
Threaten to kill B.	Beg A not to do it.
Order B to jump out of the window.	Tell A not to be so silly.
Warn B not to exceed the speed-limit.	Tell A to watch out for police cars!

Unit 74

MESSAGES

Amanda Hayward is a secretary at Standard Security Systems. Her boss, Peter Dawson, was away on business on Monday. She took several messages for him. Listen to the conversations and look at the notes.

```
MESSAGES FOR MR DAWSON - MONDAY

9.00   Jenny phoned. Won't be in
       till Friday - flu.

9.40   Mr Watkins. Can't make the
       meeting Tues. pm. Will ring Wed.

11.30  Godfrey wants Fri. off.
       Grandmother died Sun. Will
       have to go to funeral.

12.15  Wadley's Garage called. New
       car not ready yet. Strike at
       factory.

2.10   Miss Dobson (Western Video)
       must cancel order. Customers
       have changed their minds.

3.20   Mr. Gonzalez. May be in London
       21st-25th. Wants to see you
       then.

4.35   Samantha Ellis. Please phone
       her as soon as possible.
       Very urgent.

4.55   Mr Berry rang. Don't supply
       Mason and Co! Will explain
       later.
```

It's Tuesday morning. Peter Dawson has just returned to the office after his business trip to Lyon. Look at the notes and listen to her report.

Peter Good morning, Amanda. Could you come in for a minute, please?

Amanda Good morning, Mr Dawson. Did you have a good trip?

Peter Yes, thank you. Were there any messages for me yesterday?

Amanda Yes, quite a few. Shall I just run through them?

Peter Please.

Amanda Jenny phoned. She said she wouldn't be in till Friday.

Peter Oh. Why's that?

Amanda She said she had 'flu. She'd seen the doctor.

Peter Right. Go on.

Amanda Then Mr Watkins called. He said he couldn't make the meeting this afternoon but would ring you on Wednesday.

Peter OK.

Amanda Godfrey came in looking for you. He said he wanted Friday off.

Peter Did he?

Amanda Yes. He told me his grand-mother had died and he'd have to go to the funeral.

Peter Oh dear. I'd better see him later.

Amanda And Wadley's Garage called. They said your new car wasn't ready.

Peter Oh, no ... why on earth not?

Amanda They said there was a strike at the factory yesterday.

Peter Again!

Amanda After lunch Miss Dobson phoned. She said that Western Video Systems had to cancel their last order because their customers had changed their minds.

Peter Pity!

Amanda Mr Gonzalez called from Mexico to say he might be in London from 21st – 25th. He said he wanted to see you then.

Peter Oh, good. I hope he can make it.

Amanda Then a lady phoned. Samantha Ellis. She asked you to phone her as soon as possible. She said it was urgent.

Peter Ah, Samantha. I wonder what she wants.

Amanda Oh and just before five, Mr Berry phoned. He told us not to supply Mason & Co. until further notice. He said it was important and that he would explain later.

Peter Anything else?

Amanda No. That's it. Coffee?

Peter Please. That would be nice.

Exercise

Janice Taylor is personal assistant to Heather Bates, who is the chief fashion buyer for Sparks & Fraser, a chain of department stores. Heather was away yesterday visiting a supplier in Manchester. Janice took these messages.

```
Messages

9.10   Mr. Foster. Wants to see you Wed.
       Will be here at 10am.

10.25  Alan Moore, International Denim.
       Can't supply order for jeans. Their
       shipment from Hong Kong hasn't arrived.

11.05  Madame Bourvil called from Paris.
       She's sending photos of spring
       collection.

12.10  Miss Norris, Brighton store, rang.
       Monogram blouses are selling very
       well. Has nearly run out of stock.
       Wants 1000 as soon as possible.

13.45  Angela called. Got back from
       Florence yesterday. Saw lots of
       interesting things. Will discuss
       possible purchases.

14.50  Mr. Collins Wigan Textiles.
       May be able to supply new
       pullover range. Can't confirm
       order yet. Must discuss
       prices.
```

Janice reported the messages to Heather.

9.10 *Mr Foster called. He said he wanted to see you on Wednesday and that he would be here at ten o'clock.*

Report the other messages.

Look at this

am/is → was	'It's important.' She said (that) it was important.
are → were	'They're going to be late.' She said (that) they were going to be late.
have/has → had	'I've done the letters.' She said (that) she had done the letters.
don't → didn't	'I don't know.' She said (that) she didn't know.
want → wanted	'I want a day off.' She said (that) she wanted a day off.
didn't do → hadn't done	'I didn't finish it.' She said (that) she hadn't finished it.
saw → had seen	'I saw him.' She said (that) she had seen him.
was/were → had been	'I wasn't there.' She said (that) she hadn't been there.
will/won't → would/wouldn't	'I won't do it.' She said (that) she wouldn't do it.
can/can't → could/couldn't	'I can't do it.' She said (that) she couldn't do it.
may → might	'I may do it.' She said (that) she might do it.
had done/would/ could/should/ ought/might	No change

When you are reporting, you may also need to change these words:

this → that
these → those
here → there
now → then
yesterday → the day before
tomorrow → the next day
this (week) → that (week)
last (month) → the (month) before
next (year) → the next (year)

A FEW QUESTIONS

Harry Who's there?

Grimes The police. Open up!

Harry Er ... hold on a minute. I'm in the bathroom.

Grimes Come on! Open up!

Harry Oh, Sergeant Grimes. What can I do for you? Is this a social call?

Grimes Very funny, Harry. I've got a few questions to ask you. Can I come in for a minute?

Harry Have you got a search-warrant?

Grimes No. Why? Do I need one? Have you got anything to hide then, Harry?

Harry No, no. Nothing at all. Come in. Questions, you said. Well ... fire away.

Grimes Just a routine check, Harry. That's all. Just a routine check. Were you in the Mile End Road last night?

Harry No.

Grimes Mm, hm ... have you been there recently?

Harry No, no, I haven't. Why? Has there been any trouble?

Grimes I think I'll ask the questions, Harry. Where were you last night?

Harry I was in the pub, the 'Pig and Whistle'.

Grimes Did anybody see you?

Harry Oh, yes. I've got plenty of witnesses.

Grimes Witnesses, Harry? You haven't been accused of anything ... yet. Why do you need witnesses?

Harry I don't, Sergeant. I don't. Er, I was with some of my mates.

Grimes I didn't know you had any, Harry. Who were they?

Harry Er, let me think ... Tommy Ferrett, Albert Bloggs, and ...

Grimes What, Albert 'the boot' Bloggs? I thought he was still inside.

Harry No, they let him out last week. He got two years' remission for good behaviour. Oh, yes, Sid Parker was there too.

Grimes What time did you get there, and what time did you leave?

Harry I suppose I got there about seven, and left at closing time.

Grimes Did you come straight home?

Harry Yeah.

Grimes How did you get here? Did you drive?

Harry Oh, no. I'd had a few drinks. I'd never drive under the influence of alcohol, Mr Grimes, you know me. 'Think before you drink before you drive'. That's what I always say.

Grimes Very good, Harry. Very good. By the way, is that your car outside? The red Granada?

Harry That's right. I've got all the papers. I can prove it's mine.

Grimes Nice car. Especially as you're out of work.

Harry Oh, yeah. Well, my grandmother died. Left me some money.

Grimes I see. You don't mind my asking, do you?

Harry Not at all. I mean, it's your job, isn't it?

Grimes Well, how did you get that dent in the front wing, then?

Harry Oh. It happened in a car park. I wasn't there. Someone must have run into it.

Grimes Fair enough, Harry. Well, I'll be seeing you. That's all for now.

Tommy Tommy, here.

Harry Tommy, listen. It's me, Harry. The police have just been round. It was Grimes, again. I don't think he knows anything, but he asked a lot of questions. Er ... I told him I was with you.

Tommy Bloody hell! Harry! Did you have to mention me?

Harry I'm sorry, Tommy, really I am. Look we'd better check the details in case they come to see you.

Tommy What do you mean, 'in case they come to see me'? If I know Grimes, he'll be here any minute. Come on, Harry. Tell me exactly what he asked you, and what you told him.

Exercise 1

'Can I come in for a minute?'

He asked if he could come in, so I asked him if he'd got a search-warrant.

'Where were you last night?'

He asked me where I'd been, and I told him I'd been in the pub.

Look at the conversation between Harry and Sergeant Grimes. Report all the questions and answers.

Look at this

'What's your name?'

She asked me what my name was.

'Are you married?'

She asked me if I was married.

Exercise 2

At Watermouth College of Education, students who wish to follow an examination preparation course have to have a short interview, to satisfy the college authorities that their English is good enough to follow the course. These are the notes which the examiner uses during the interview.

Practise with a partner; one is a student, the other is the examiner.

Examiner *What's your name?*

Student *My name's ....*

Watermouth College of Education
Department of English
Exam English as a Foreign Language (*Pre-course entry questionnaire*)

1 Name?

2 Nationality?

3 Home town?

4 Marital status?

5 Brothers and sisters?

6 Years of English?

7 Length of time spent in England?

8 Occupation? Tell me about it.

9 Hobbies? Tell me about them.

10 Reason for learning English?

11 Exams passed (if any)?

12 Accommodation–flat, landlady or hotel?

13 What would you do if you won £10,000?

14 Other languages?

15 What do you think about England?

16 What major differences have you noticed between England and your country?

Exercise 3

Imagine you are a student who has just had the interview. Report to a friend.

Friend *What did they ask you?*

Student *They asked me if I had any brothers or sisters. I told them I had one brother and two sisters.*

TRUST THE HEART

Melinda stood at the end of the garden, watching the sun begin to set behind the orchard into the sea beyond. She stood as she had done so many times thinking of that last quarrel two weeks before. She remembered how Damian had at first denied the affair with Tamsin, but then when she had forced him to admit it, how he had apologized and begged her for forgiveness. She sobbed a little as she thought of her harsh words, and how Damian, the only man she had ever really loved, had broken down and cried like a baby when she had refused to see him again. That was two weeks ago and she had heard nothing from him since. She had tried to telephone. She wanted to admit that she had been unjust, to tell him how much she regretted calling him a liar, she wanted to explain that she hadn't meant to hurt him.

Suddenly the noise of the garden gate opening startled her. She turned and through the gloom she thought she could make out the familiar figure of Damian. Was it him . . . ? Could it possibly be . . . ? The approaching figure stepped into the last patch of sunlight and the last rays of the setting sun illuminated his long, dark, curly hair. He stopped, unsure of himself. 'Oh, Damian,' she called softly. 'Damian, is it really you?'

'Melinda,' he murmured, 'My Melinda!'

She sighed deeply and ran to greet him.

She took his hands tightly in hers. 'My darling,' she whispered, 'Can you ever forgive me?'

'We must never speak of it again,' he replied.

'But Damian, I never meant . . . ,'

He interrupted her, 'It's all right. I know that now. My darling, promise me something?'

'Anything!' she cried.

'Here, this is for you. Please, please accept it, and wear it forever.' He drew a small leather box from his pocket and leaned forward to give it to her. Suddenly the box fell from his grasp. He bent to pick it up and at that moment his glasses slipped from his nose.

'Blast! Now where have they gone? I can't see a thing without them,' he explained. Melinda went to help him. There was a crunch as his foot crushed the glasses into the gravel path. 'Oh, no, now I've trodden on them!' he exclaimed. 'Why can't I do anything right? Why do I always ruin everything?'

Her laughter pealed round the garden. 'Oh, Damian, you silly boy, that's why I love you so much!'

Exercise

Here are some notes about what happened on page 32 of 'Trust the heart', when Melinda and Damian met for the first time at a party. Read the notes and construct their conversation.

Mrs Blaze introduced her to Damian. *'Oh, Melinda . . . I'd like you to meet Damian.'*

Continue.

1 They greeted each other.
2 He offered to get her a drink.
3 She thanked him, and asked him to get her a dry sherry.
4 He brought her a martini, and apologized because they'd run out of sherry.
5 She replied that it didn't matter, and told him not to worry about it.
6 He asked her if she would like to dance, and she accepted.
7 He said how much he liked the music and she agreed.
8 He complimented her on her dress, and she thanked him, and added that she had made it herself.
9 He invited her to watch the sunset on the terrace, and she accepted.
10 He suggested dinner the next evening.
11 She agreed and promised to meet him.
12 He suggested 'The Old Stable' restaurant and explained that the owner was an old school friend.
13 He arranged to collect her at eight o'clock.

Unit 77

WEDDINGS

Listen to two people talking about their weddings.
Adrian had a traditional church wedding. Ann was married in a registry office.
Compare their weddings with customs and traditions in your country.
Tell the story of the wedding in the pictures.

History

Two thousand years ago the British Isles were inhabited by speakers of Celtic languages. These languages still survive in parts of Wales, Scotland, Ireland, and Brittany in France. The Celts were conquered by the Romans, and from 43 BC to about AD 410 the areas which are now England and Wales were part of the Roman Empire, and Latin was the language of government. Between the fourth and seventh centuries A.D., the Anglo-Saxons arrived from what is now northern Germany, Holland and Denmark, and occupied most of England, and parts of southern Scotland. In some parts of Wales, Scotland and Ireland, people still speak Celtic languages. The Anglo-Saxons spoke a Germanic language which forms the basis of modern English. This language was modified by the arrival of Viking invaders in the north and east of the country, who came from Norway and Denmark between the eighth and eleventh centuries. These Scandinavian settlers spoke Old Norse, which was related to Anglo-Saxon, and which is the parent language of modern Danish. The mixing of the two languages greatly enriched the vocabulary of English. By the middle of the tenth century England had become a unified country under one king.

In 1066 England was conquered by the French-speaking Normans, and French became the language of government. For the next three hundred years three languages co-existed. The aristocracy spoke French, the ordinary people spoke English, while Latin was used in the church. Modern English evolved from the mingling of the three tongues. Today English vocabulary is approximately half Germanic (from the Saxons and Vikings) and half Romance (from French and Latin). There are however considerable borrowings from other languages.

Some derived words

Old English	shirt, life, death, heaven, earth, love, hate
Old Norse	skirt, birth, window, ugly, wrong, they, their, them
French	boil, roast, veal, beef, pork, village, painter, tailor
Latin	index, item, major, memorandum

THE ENGLISH LANGUAGE

Features of the English language

English has changed so much in the last 1500 years that it would now be hardly recognizable to the Anglo-Saxons who brought the language across the North Sea. Although they would be able to recognize many individual words, they would not recognize the way those words are put together to make sentences. Old English, like modern German, was a highly inflected language, i.e. most words changed their endings or forms to show their relationship to other words in the sentence according to number (singular, plural), gender (masculine, feminine, neuter), case (subject, object), tense (past, future) etc. Some modern English words still inflect, but much less so than in other European languages. The English verb 'to ride' inflects into five forms (ride, rides, riding, rode, ridden) whereas the equivalent German verb has sixteen forms. The English word 'the' has only one form, whereas other European languages would have several different forms. The trend towards simplicity of form is considered to be a strength of English. Another strength is the flexibility of function of individual words. Look at these uses of the word 'round':

There was a *round* table. (adjective)

He bought a *round* of drinks. (noun)

He turned *round*. (adverb)

He ran *round* the field. (preposition)

The car tried to *round* the bend too quickly. (verb)

This flexibility, together with a flexibility towards the assimilation of words borrowed from other languages and the spontaneous creation

of new words have made English what it is today, an effective medium of international communication. English has achieved this in spite of the difficulties caused by written English, which is not systematically phonetic.

Some loan words

Arabic	*admiral, algebra, mattress*
Spanish	*mosquito, cigar, canyon*
Italian	*piano, violin, spaghetti*
Dutch	*yacht, boss, deck*
Hindi	*pyjamas, shampoo, bungalow*
Turkish	*yoghurt, kiosk*
Japanese	*tycoon, karate*
Malay	*bamboo, compound*
Nahuatl (Aztec)	*tomato, chocolate*
Quechua (Inca)	*coca, quinine*
Hungarian	*coach, paprika*
Classical Greek	*theatre, astronomy, logic*
Gaelic	*whisky*
Russian	*vodka, sputnik*
Finnish	*sauna*
Chinese	*tea, silk*
Portuguese	*marmalade*
Eskimo	*anorak*
Czech	*robot*
Farsi (Iranian)	*lilac*
Basque	*bizarre*
Carib	*canoe*
Australian Aborigine	*kangaroo boomerang*
Modern French	*rendezvous, café*
Modern German	*kindergarten*

Some 'created' words

xerox, to xerox, xeroxed
a hoover, to hoover, hoovered
mackintosh, sandwich, submarine, helicopter, pop, rock'n roll, x-ray, astronaut, hot dog.

English today

Approximately 350 million people speak English as their first language. About the same number use it as a second language. It is the language of aviation, international sport and pop music. 75% of the world's mail is in English, 60% of the world's radio stations broadcast in English and more than half of the world's periodicals are printed in English. It is an official language in 44 countries. In many others it is the language of business, commerce and technology. There are many varieties of English, but Scottish, Texan, Australian, Indian and Jamaican speakers of English, in spite of the differences in pronunciation, structure and vocabulary, would recognize that they are all speaking the same basic language.

DEPARTURES

Gina has been studying English at a language school in England. Her course finishes at the end of this week and she's returning home on Saturday. She's in a travel agency now.

Travel agent Take a seat, please. I'll be with you in a minute. Yes, what can I do for you?

Gina I want to fly to Rome. Are there any seats available on Saturday?

Travel agent Just a moment and I'll check ... Rome ... what time of day are you thinking of going?

Gina Well, I'd rather not arrive too late. How about late morning or early afternoon?

Travel agent The 12.10's fully booked, I'm afraid. There are seats available on the 14.55 or the 16.30. Is that too late for you?

Gina The 14.55 sounds OK. What time does that get in?

Travel agent 18.15 local time; there's a one hour time difference, you know.

Gina OK. That'll be fine. I'll pay cash but I'll have to go to the bank and come back.

Travel agent That's all right. I'll hold the reservation for you.

Streamline Taxis Streamline Taxis.

Gina I'd like to book a taxi for Saturday morning, please.

Streamline Taxis Where are you going?

Gina London Airport, Heathrow. There'll be three of us sharing. How much will it be?

Streamline Taxis £35.

Gina £35! Each or between us?

Streamline Taxis Oh, that's all together. What time do you want to leave?

Gina The check-in time is five to two but I don't know how long it takes to get there.

Streamline Taxis Well we'd better pick you up about half eleven, in case we hit traffic. Can I have your name and address?

Gina Yes. It's Gina Castelli ... two 'I's. 32, Seaport Road.

Streamline Taxis 32, Seaport Road. OK. 11.30 Saturday morning. Thank you.

Mr Jenkins Come in!

Gina Oh, hello, Mr Jenkins.

Mr Jenkins Hello, Gina. What can I do for you?

Gina I've just come to say goodbye.

Mr Jenkins Oh yes, of course. You're leaving, aren't you? When?

Gina I'm flying tomorrow morning. I'm back at work on Monday morning.

Mr Jenkins Well, I must say Gina, we'll be sorry to lose you.

Gina I don't really want to go but ... well, I just wanted to thank you and all the other teachers.

Mr Jenkins Oh, that's all right, Gina.

Gina I've really learnt a lot. I hope to come back next year ... for a holiday.

Mr Jenkins Don't forget to send us a card, and if you do come back, call in and see us.

Gina No, I won't forget.

Mr Jenkins Well, there's the bell. Goodbye then, and have a safe journey.

Gina Goodbye and thanks for everything.

Gina Jacques! I'm glad I haven't missed you.

Jacques Hello, Gina. When are you leaving?

Gina Tomorrow morning. I don't suppose I'll see you again. So, goodbye. It was nice meeting you.

Jacques And you. But you will keep in touch, won't you?

Gina Yes, I will. You've got my address, haven't you?

Jacques Yes, and remember, if you're ever in Cherbourg, give me a call. I'd be so pleased to see you again.

Gina Oh, I will. You can be sure of that. And you must do the same if you're ever in Rome.

Jacques Well. Goodbye then.

Gina Goodbye ... and look after yourself.

Mrs Sharples Gina! The taxi's outside. Are you ready? Have you got everything?

Gina Yes, thank you, Mrs Sharples. And ... thank you again.

Mrs Sharples Thank you, Gina, for the flowers. Now don't forget to phone us when you get home. Just to let us know that you've arrived safely.

Gina No, I won't forget. I don't know whether I'll be able to phone tonight or not, but in any case, I'll ring you in the morning whatever happens.

Mrs Sharples Well, goodbye then, dear. You'd better not keep the taxi waiting. Have a nice trip. Bye-bye.

Gina Bye. And look after yourselves. And thank Mr Sharples for me.

APPENDIX

Material recorded on cassette but not included in the text of the units is printed below.

Unit 1

1 The train now standing at Platform 5 will be the 10.25 to Exeter St David's, calling at Reading, Pewsey, Westbury and Taunton.
2 The train now standing at Platform 3 is the 10.20 Inter-City service to Bristol.
3 The train now arriving at Platform 2 is the 9.12 from Oxford.
4 The next train leaving from Platform 9 will be the 10.25 Inter-City service to Plymouth and Penzance. The train will be divided at Plymouth. Passengers for stations to Penzance should take the front six carriages.
5 The train now arriving at Platform 12 is the 7.10 from Swansea. Trains from Swansea are running approximately 15 minutes late due to maintenance work between Swansea and Cardiff.

Unit 13

A Airport announcements

1 This is the last call for the twelve o'clock British Airways flight BA 412 to Amsterdam. Would passengers for this flight please proceed without delay to Gate 17.
2 Scandinavian Airlines announce the departure of the 12.05 flight SK 526 to Stockholm. This flight is now boarding at Gate 8.
3 Would passengers for the 12.10 Iberia flight IB 341 to Madrid please go at once to Gate 16 where this flight is now boarding.
4 Alitalia regret to announce that their 12.15 flight AZ 281 to Rome will be delayed for approximately 30 minutes.
5 Olympic Airways announce the departure of the 12.30 flight OA 260 to Athens. Would passengers on this flight please proceed to Gate 19.
6 This is a call for Mr Gaston Meyer. Would Mr Gaston Meyer travelling on the 12.45 Sabena flight SN 604 to Brussels report to the airport information desk, please.

B In-flight announcements

1 Good afternoon, ladies and gentlemen. Captain Perez and his crew welcome you aboard Iberia flight IB 341 to Madrid. I am sorry to announce a slight delay. We are still waiting for clearance from Air Traffic Control. The delay won't be too long and we hope to arrive in Madrid on time.
2 This is your captain speaking. We are now passing over the English coast. Our Boeing 727 is cruising at a height of 30,000 feet and our speed is approximately 560 miles per hour. The temperature in Madrid is 18°C and it is a clear and sunny day. We expect to pass through some slight turbulence and would recommend passengers to remain in their seats and keep their belts fastened.
3 We are now beginning our descent to Madrid. Would passengers please make sure that their seat-belts are fastened and extinguish all smoking materials. We would like to remind passengers that smoking is not permitted until you are in the airport building.

4 We hope you had a pleasant and enjoyable flight. We would like to thank you for travelling on Iberia, and we hope to see you again soon. Would passengers please remain seated until the plane has come to a complete stop and the doors have been opened.

Unit 15

Bargaining

Lucy Excuse me.
Stallholder Yes, miss?
Lucy How much do you want for this plate?
Stallholder Let me see. Oh, yes ... that's a lovely example of Victorian brass. It's worth twenty quid.
Lucy Twenty pounds! Oh, that's too much for me. It's a pity. It's really nice.
Stallholder Ah, I said it's worth twenty quid. I'm only asking fifteen for it.
Lucy Fifteen pounds?
Stallholder Yes. It's a real bargain.
Lucy Oh, I'm sure it is ... but I can't afford that!
Stallholder Well, look ... just for you ... I'll make it fourteen quid. I can't go any lower than that.
Lucy I'll give you ten.
Stallholder Ten! Come on, love. You must be joking! I paid more than that for it myself! Fourteen. It's worth every penny.
Lucy Well, perhaps I could give you eleven.
Stallholder Thirteen. That's my final offer.
Lucy Twelve.
Stallholder Twelve fifty?
Lucy All right, twelve fifty.
Stallholder There you are, love. You've got a real bargain there!
Lucy Yes, thank you very much.

Unit 44

1
Our six finalists are No 14 Miss Lancashire, No 13 Miss Dorset, Miss Norfolk No 50, Miss Gwent No 6, No 30 Miss Strathclyde and Miss Warwickshire No 40. Would the first contestant please come forward.

2
Announcer This is 17-year-old Grace Field from Lancashire. Just stand there, Grace. You're a shop-assistant, aren't you?
Grace Field Yes, I am.
Announcer What kind of shop is it?
Grace Field It's a clothes shop. We sell children's clothes. It's only a temporary job, actually.
Announcer Now, first of all: what do you do in your spare time?
Grace Field Well, I like dressmaking, I make all my own clothes ... and cooking. I do a lot of cooking.
Announcer That's a beautiful dress you're wearing, did you make it?
Grace Field Yes, with a little help from my mother.

Announcer Now, Grace. You said your job was a temporary one. What would you really like to do?
Grace Field Oh, to work with children. Definitely.
Announcer Uh huh. Last question. If you could have one wish, what would it be?
Grace Field I've thought about that a lot ... world peace.
Announcer Thank you, Grace.

3
Announcer Our next contestant is a beauty consultant from Dorset, Victoria Hardy. Victoria's 25. Hello, Victoria.
Victoria Hardy Good evening, Terry. It's lovely to meet you.
Announcer Mmm. Thank you. Have you got any great ambitions, Victoria?
Victoria Hardy Yes. I'd like to sail across the Atlantic.
Announcer The Atlantic! Alone?
Victoria Hardy No, no.
Announcer Have you any experience of sailing?
Victoria Hardy Yes, I go sailing every weekend.
Announcer Is that your only hobby?
Victoria Hardy It's my favourite one, but I like horseriding too.
Announcer Good. Good. What about one wish?
Victoria Hardy I'd wish for a long life.
Announcer Very nice. Thank you very much, Victoria.

4
Announcer The third finalist is Lynn King, a primary school teacher from Norfolk. You look too young to be a teacher, Lynn. None of my teachers looked like you.
Lynn King I'm 21, this is my first year.
Announcer I see. Tell me about your hobbies.
Lynn King I'm very interested in astronomy ... and playing the piano.
Announcer Ah, music and the stars! How very interesting! Have you got any great ambitions?
Lynn King You'll laugh ... but my ambition is to go to the moon ... seriously.
Announcer Do you think you ever will?
Lynn King Who knows?
Announcer And if you could make a wish?
Lynn King I'd just wish for happiness.

5
Announcer Next we have Myfanwy Lloyd, a nineteen year old brunette from Gwent in Wales. What do you do, Myfanwy?
Myfanwy Lloyd No , Myfanwy. We pronounce it 'Myfanwy'. I'm still at university.
Announcer What are you studying?
Myfanwy Lloyd Drama ... it's also my hobby.
Announcer Any other hobbies, Myfanwy?
Myfanwy Lloyd Well, I'm a black belt in judo.
Announcer Oh, dear ... I'd better pronounce your name correctly, hadn't I?
Myfanwy Lloyd It's all right.
Announcer What do you hope to do when you leave university?
Myfanwy Lloyd To be an actress.

Announcer I'm sure you'll be successful. Would you like to make a wish?

Myfanwy Lloyd Yes. I'd wish for health ... I think it's the most important thing in life.

6

Announcer Our next finalist, from Scotland, is Miss Strathclyde, a twenty-three year old fashion model ... Dawn Munro. Hello, Dawn.

Dawn Munro Hello, Terry.

Announcer What are your interests?

Dawn Munro Er ... dancing ... and ... er ... photographic work.

Announcer So you're a keen amateur photographer?

Dawn Munro No, no ... I'm more interested in modelling.

Announcer I see. What about your ambitions?

Dawn Munro I'd like to become Miss World.

Announcer Really? You are ambitious, aren't you? And your wish?

Dawn Munro I've always wanted one thing ... fame ... I'd like to see my face on magazine covers.

Announcer Well, it's certainly pretty enough. Thank you, Dawn.

7

Announcer Finally, Kerry Talbot ... Miss Warwickshire. How old are you, Kerry?

Kerry Talbot Eighteen.

Announcer Don't be nervous. Speak up a bit. And do you work?

Kerry Talbot I'm a typist.

Announcer What do you like doing in your free time?

Kerry Talbot Reading ... I like reading ... and swimming.

Announcer What's your ambition?

Kerry Talbot To have a large family. I love children.

Announcer And if you had one wish, what would you ask for?

Kerry Talbot It sounds silly, but I'd ask for good luck. I'm very superstitious. Look ... my fingers are crossed.

Announcer Thank you, Kerry. Now while our judges are making their final decision, we'll take a short break.

8

Announcer Now, here to announce the results of our contest is Mr Derek Chorley, the Chairman of EBC. Mr Chorley ...

Derek Chorley Thank you, Terry. I'm going to read the results in reverse order. Third, for a prize of £5,000 and a weekend in Paris, is Number 13, Victoria Hardy from Dorset! Second, with a prize of £10,000 and a holiday in Spain, is Number 6 ... Myfanwy Lloyd! And now ... Miss Britain ... with a holiday in California and £20,000 ... yes, £20,000 is ... Number 30 ... Dawn Munro from Strathclyde!

Unit 52

Donna

Well, she's quite a lively, talkative person in her ... in her late teens. She's fairly tall with a ... a good figure. She's got a heart-shaped face with a small, sort of turned-up nose. It's very attractive really. She's got long, black wavy hair and er ... blue eyes with very long eyelashes. Her complexion is ... well, she's olive-skinned. Her lips are very full ... and she's got dimples ... dimples in her cheeks.

Colin

He's a very big guy, you know, well-built with very broad shoulders. Not fat, really, really ... just well-built. He's in his early thirties. He's got a long face with thin lips. Oh, and a small scar on his chin. He's got very short, fair hair but with long sideburns and a moustache. Eyes ... I haven't really noticed the colour, he wears glasses. He's got thick eyebrows and a kind of a long, straight nose. He's fairly reserved, thoughtful, sometimes even moody.

Janet

She's sophisticated. Well-dressed, expensive hairstyle and so on. I'd say she was in her late thirties or early forties, but she looks younger. She's about average height and very slim. Her hair's very blonde, dyed, I think, but I'm not sure about that. It's always very neat, not long. She's got pale grey eyes with thin eyebrows. Her face is always sunburned and very well made up. It's an attractive face ... not really beautiful, but very attractive, you know what I mean. High cheekbones, small chin ... oh and yes, there's a beauty spot on her left cheek. She's a very calm and reliable sort of person, very sociable and always very, very polite.

Robert

Robert's a wonderful person really. He's elderly but not old ... still very lively and amusing. He's probably in his early seventies. He's got white hair, receding a bit, and a small white beard. He's medium build, a little overweight perhaps. He's got very nice, large, brown eyes and he always seems to be smiling ... lots of wrinkles round the eyes, laughter lines I think you call them. He's got a very high, lined forehead which makes him look very intelligent, which he is, of course.

Unit 65

Mr Williams Good morning, doctor.

Doctor Hello, Mr Williams. Take a seat. What seems to be the trouble?

Mr Williams I'm not sure, doctor. But I haven't been feeling too well. I think I must have a touch of flu.

Doctor Mm. There's a lot of it going round at the moment. What are the symptoms?

Mr Williams I'm feeling very tired, and I'm aching all over. I've been sneezing a lot, and feeling pretty feverish, hot and cold all the time. Oh, and I've got a sore throat.

Doctor Any vomiting?

Mr Williams No, but I don't feel very hungry. I've got no appetite at all.

Doctor Well, let's have a look at you. Open your mouth. 'Aah.' Yes, your throat's a bit inflamed, and the glands in your neck are swollen. Can you just unbutton your shirt? I want to listen to your chest. Breathe deeply. Right. I'll just take your temperature. Don't say anything for a minute, just keep the thermometer under your tongue. I'll write out a prescription for you, but you know the best thing is just to go home, go to bed, and take plenty of fluids.

Unit 72

Estate Agent I'm afraid it's been rather neglected. The present owner is in his eighties. He's just gone into an old people's home.

Robin Yes. It looks as though a lot needs doing to it.

Estate Agent That's true, but the price is very

reasonable. It would be ideal for a do-it-yourself man.

Robin Mm. I'm not very good with my hands, I'm afraid. We'd have to get most things done for us, wouldn't we, Jean?

Jean Oh, I don't know. Could we see inside?

Estate Agent Of course. I'll show you the kitchen first.

Jean Oh dear! Just look at that sink. It must have been there since the house was built.

Robin It's a nice large room, though, and there's plenty of light. We'd have to have kitchen units put in, and we'd need to get it tiled.

Jean But you could do the ceiling yourself, couldn't you? And the painting.

Robin Is that the only power-point there?

Estate Agent I'm afraid so.

Robin It looks pretty old. I'm sure the whole place would need rewiring. We certainly couldn't do that ourselves and we'd need to have more points put in at the same time.

Estate Agent Would you like to see the lounge? It's through here.

Jean Oh my God! It'd certainly need redecorating. I suppose we could do the painting and wallpapering. What's it like upstairs?

Estate Agent Pretty bad, really. It obviously hasn't been decorated for years, and as I told you on the phone, it hasn't got a bathroom. But you could have the small bedroom converted into a bathroom and get a grant towards the cost. All the other houses in the street have had that done.

Robin What about the toilet?

Estate Agent I'm afraid that's outside, but you could get one put in the new bathroom. And of course, you'd get a grant for that as well.

Jean Is there anything else that needs doing?

Estate Agent Well, you'd probably have to get the roof repaired pretty soon.

Robin The sooner the better if you ask me. It looks as though water's been coming in over there. And, of course, we'd want to have central heating put in, and the windows double glazed, it's a very noisy street. I couldn't do any of that myself.

Estate Agent Of course not.

Robin Anyway, thank you for showing us around. But really I think the best thing would be to knock it down and start all over again!

Unit 75

9.00

Amanda Mr Dawson's office.

Jenny Oh, it's Jenny. Can you give Mr Dawson a message? I won't be in till Friday, I've got flu. I saw the doctor this morning.

Amanda OK, Jenny. I'll pass the message on. I hope you feel better soon.

9.40

Amanda Mr Dawson's office. Can I help you?

Mr Watkins May I speak to Mr Dawson, please?

Amanda I'm afraid he's away on business. He'll be back tomorrow. Can I take a message?

Mr Watkins Please. It's Tom Watkins here. Look, I can't make the meeting on Tuesday afternoon. Something important's come up. I'll ring Peter on Wednesday.

11.30

Amanda Hello, Godfrey. What can I do for you?

Godfrey Mr Dawson isn't here, is he?

Amanda No, not till tomorrow.
Godfrey Ah … it's just that I want Friday off. You see, my grandmother died yesterday. I'll have to go to the funeral.
Amanda Oh, I am sorry. How old was she?
Godfrey 92.

12.15
Amanda Mr Dawson's office.
Salesman Can you put me through to Mr Dawson?
Amanda I'm afraid he isn't here today. Would you like to leave a message?
Salesman Oh, right. Wadley's Garage here. It's about his new car. It isn't ready yet. There's a strike at the factory today.

2.10
Amanda Good afternoon. Mr Dawson's office.
Miss Dobson Good afternoon. This is Juliet Dobson from Western Video Systems. Mr Dawson's at the trade fair in Lyon, isn't he?
Amanda Yes, that's right. He should be here tomorrow.
Miss Dobson Well, can you give him this message first thing in the morning? I'm afraid we must cancel our last order. The customers have changed their minds, again!

3.20
Amanda Good afternoon. Mr Dawson's office.
Mr Gonzalez Hello, this is Miguel Gonzalez speaking. Is Peter there?
Amanda No, I'm afraid he's away on business today. Can I pass on a message, Señor Gonzalez?
Mr Gonzalez Yes. I may be in London from the 21st to the 25th. I want to see Peter then, if possible. It's about the agency in Mexico.

4.35
Amanda Mr Dawson's office.
Mrs Ellis My name's Samantha Ellis. Can you get Mr Dawson to phone me as soon as he gets back from Lyon? It really is very urgent.

4.55
Amanda Mr Dawson's office.
Mr Berry Ah, Miss Hayward. This is Charles Berry.
Amanda Oh, good afternoon, sir.
Mr Berry I've got an important message for Mr Dawson. Give it to him the minute he comes in. Just say, 'Don't supply Mason and Company until further notice'. I'll explain later.

Unit 78

A church wedding
Adrian and Caroline were married recently.

'Our wedding was a pretty typical one, really. Caroline and I met about three years ago, and we got engaged last summer. We both wanted a traditional wedding. I suppose it's expensive, and some people say it's a waste of money, but it is a day to remember all your life. Anyway, we wanted to please our parents, and we both wanted to get married in church. Caroline's father hired a white Rolls-Royce to bring her to the church, we wanted the whole works! You know, top hat, tails, champagne – the full treatment. The men rented their morning suits for the day. Caroline had three bridesmaids – her sister and two of her cousins, and a page. The page was her nephew. He's only three and he made a lot of noise during the ceremony. I didn't feel my best that day because my stag party went on until five o'clock in the morning. I do remember the photographs, though. We seemed to be waiting around for ages. Although it was a very sunny Saturday – it was in May – there was a pretty cold wind. The reception was at the Carlton Hotel, it must have cost Caroline's dad a packet. The speeches went on a bit too long, I think … and of course some of them were a bit vulgar, but I suppose that's a tradition. It took twenty minutes just to read out all the telegrams. I'd been very careful, and I'd parked my car round the corner, but of course they somehow managed to find out where it was. You should have seen what they'd done to it! It was covered with lipstick, and they'd tied cans to the bumper. But anyway, they didn't find out where we were having our honeymoon. We went to Scotland.'

A registry office wedding
Stuart and Ann were married in a registry office.

'Stuart and I met last year. We were both working in Birmingham, although Stuart comes from Leeds and I'm from London. We didn't want an elaborate wedding and neither of us are particularly religious, so we got married in the registry office. Another thing is that neither of our families are very well off, and it seemed silly to go to all the expense, when you need the money to set up a new home. We just invited our parents and a couple of friends, who were the witnesses. It was all very simple. We didn't have a reception or anything. We just had a few drinks round at our place. We didn't even bother with a cake. We didn't have a honeymoon, because Stuart's just started his own business and we couldn't afford the time.'